MISSISSIPPI MISADVENTURE

Paul Stutzman

ISBN 13: 978-0-9998874-4-8

Remembering Jonah,

who also took a boat trip he shouldn't have.

God sent him a whale and sent me a bus, and

He didn't give up on either of us.

From the Author

Please note that this account of my Mississippi River journey appeared previously, combined with my hike of the Camino de Santiago in Spain and published as the first edition of *Stuck in the Weeds.* We have separated the two adventures. *Mississippi Misadventure* is now the account of attempting to kayak the Mississippi River, and the hike in Spain appears in another book under the title of *Pilgrims.*

A special thanks to Ivan and Fran for transporting me to the headwaters of the Mississippi River and abandoning me in a vast swamp. Thanks to Dave for rescuing me from that river.

Thank you to my editor, Elaine Starner, for her tireless assistance in bringing this book about.

To see my daily blogs on the Mississippi and additional photos of other adventures, you are welcome to visit my website at www.paulstutzman.com.

You can also visit me on Facebook at Paul Stutzman Author for updates and random musings.

Introduction

This adventure started as all my adventures do—with a thought.

Of course, many folks have many thoughts about many things they want to do in life. Too often the process stops right there, in the mind.

A thought is just that, a thought. It may be fleeting—only a flash through the synapses of one's brain—or it may be a thought that, given incubation time, expands and strengthens into an idea. The idea then roams the chambers of the mind until finally reaching a door marked *Choice*. And there, it waits.

For the person attached to the mind we've been peering into, opening this door is the tipping point between a mundane existence and unimaginable adventure into the unknown. People seem to forget that they have the power to open that door or leave it tightly closed.

We so often hear the lament, "I don't have a choice." I really believe that for some folks this has become a mantra that defines and inhibits their lives. They live as though that door marked *Choice* has a menacing sign hanging on it saying, DO NOT TOUCH, and they resign themselves to never even trying the latch and testing whether or not it is locked.

I'm here to say that we do have the power of choice. We can make any choice we want. It may be a wrong or foolish choice, but nevertheless, that power resides in us.

When the idea of a kayaking trip down the Mississippi River began to lurk behind that door in my mind, I gave it the room and freedom to feed and grow. There was even a new book title attached to this idea—it would be *Paddling Through*.

Other adventures were behind me: a thru-hike of the Appalachian Trail and a biking trip across the continental United States. Books had followed each of those adventures, and my new life as an author consisted of writing, speaking engagements, and book signings. But I too easily slip into comfortable routines that do not stretch me. I reach a point of stagnation, mentally, spiritually, even physically. I find that I need new excitement and growth, and those come not from talking about past adventures but in the actual engagement of new challenges.

I was at just such a point of needing to challenge nature once again when the idea for paddling the entire Mississippi River made its appearance in my mind and waited for my hand on the door marked *Choice*.

And eventually, I opened the door.

Chapter 1

One final thrust from my graphite racing paddle confirmed my fears. The entrapment was complete.

The swamp grasses of the upper Mississippi River had my kayak—and me with it—firmly ensnared in the deep weeds. Like Moses in the bulrushes, my vessel and I were out of sight, ensconced in cattails, duckweed, skunk cabbage, and prairie cord grass. More unknown foliage loomed overhead, admiring the latest captive. I was hemmed in fore and aft, port and starboard, and held fast. I was going nowhere.

Very few humans are brave enough or foolish enough to navigate the first 150 miles of the mighty Mississippi River. According to statistics kept at the visitor center in Bemidji, Minnesota, when I arrived at the river's headwaters in the late summer of 2013, only six other people had made the attempt that year.

If a person successfully navigates through the swamp that meanders for over 60 miles, other dangers await. Downstream lurks a section of several miles where fallen trees in the river render navigation nearly impossible. Battling through and emerging from that maze, one comes face-to-face with thousands of acres of wild rice fields. The huge rice paddy awaits its turn to befuddle and discourage the paddler.

I'd been paddling downstream, but my kayak was pointed north. Wait—shouldn't this mighty river draining parts of 31 states be flowing *south*? Or was I already lost and paddling in the wrong direction? The reality is that for the first 60 miles the Mississippi River flows (or, shall I say, *stagnates)* in a swamp that extends north to Bemidji, Minnesota, where the river flows into Lake Bemidji. Then, as it leaves the lake, the Mississippi changes direction and turns toward the south on its route to the Gulf of Mexico. Past the swamp, the rice paddy, and the first big lake, there are more frightful lakes. How I dreaded those. But that was yet ahead. Now, I was stuck in the weeds of this swamp.

Unless I could extricate myself from my current predicament, I would fall 2,335 miles short of my goal—to paddle the entire Mississippi River from its source at Lake Itasca to the delta in the Gulf of Mexico. Many paddlers have traversed the Mississippi River, but most conclude their journey in New Orleans, Louisiana. The official end of the Mississippi River is another 100 miles beyond that city. Mile Zero of the river is an area known as "Head of the Passes." Here the waters of the mighty Mississippi empty into the Gulf of Mexico, ending a journey that bisects America from north to south.

Already, less than two miles into my quest, the possibility of reaching my goal seemed futile. On this very first day, I was wondering if I was chasing a doomed dream.

Giving in to frustration, anger, and a bit of fear—make that *a lot* of fear—I slammed the paddle onto the deck of my kayak. How had I gotten myself into such a mess once again? What was I doing here?

I was stuck in these weeds, a prisoner in the kayak-eating, merciless swamp. My life might very possibly end here, and I'd be food for the swamp rodents.

Imprisoned in my kayak, disgusted with my predicament, and nursing twinges of self-pity, I leaned back and—I frankly admit—wondered if this choice I had made was perhaps the most foolish, ill-advised choice of my entire life.

Chapter 2

In grade school, I had read a book about Tom Sawyer and Huckleberry Finn. Their river-rafting trip seemed so peaceful and quaint. What young boy hasn't dreamed about skipping school, escaping family and society, and floating away on an adventure? Mark Twain put fantasies of drifting down the Mississippi River into my boyhood head, and those thoughts had never left.

However, I was no longer a boy, and I should have realized that things aren't always as idyllic as they seem.

I did have some limited experience in a kayak. That, too, had left a charming, serene vision in my head and had given me unrealistic expectations. My first kayaking adventure had been soon after 911; and that fact, in itself, might have added to the appeal. I floated down the Colorado River, far removed from talk of terror and trouble.

Because of the recent attack on the Twin Towers, security was very tight. I had signed on with an outfitter. After filling out various forms, the guides took us down a small, winding private road to the base of Hoover Dam. The great concrete span loomed above us as our small group received brief instructions and then put our crafts into the waters of the Colorado River that flow through Black Canyon, on the border between Arizona and Nevada.

Although there were only a handful of kayakers and two guides, we were essentially turned loose on the river. Each paddler moved along at their own speed, stopping whenever and wherever each individual desired. The high cliffs of the canyon offered side creeks, caves, waterfalls, and hot springs to explore, and the guides had given us information on where these could be found. I did stop at one point, climbed an aluminum ladder over a small waterfall, and hiked to a hot spring where I had my lunch. Our only firm directive was that we get ourselves (and our kayaks) twelve miles down the river to a place called Willow Beach by a certain time that afternoon. The outfitter would pick us up there and return us to our vehicles.

I started off tentatively, but it didn't take long until I relaxed more and began to enjoy myself. The flow of water through the canyon is controlled by the dam, and that morning, the river was peaceful and serene. I caught sight of mountain goats on the cliffs and watched for eagles and hawks gliding on the currents high above. At one point, all other kayakers were out of sight. I felt completely alone there on the calm water, drifting between the walls of the canyon. I laid my paddle across the front of the kayak and dangled my sandaled feet along the sides of the bow, letting my craft float along as I took in the grandeur.

A mallard duck flew just above the surface of the water, coming straight toward me. I could see the shimmering green colors of its head and hear the soft *whoosh* of its wings as the tips grazed the water. That image is still clear in my mind. I thought, *This is just amazing. Could there be a more peaceful moment?*

As I thought about an adventure on the Mississippi, I hoped to duplicate that scene. Of course, by now I also have learned that such moments can never be duplicated. Savor them when they occur.

As I had considered my choice of the Mississippi for my next adventure, a complication arose.

Every year, my sisters and numerous cousins and friends charter a bus and take a trip together. From one year to the next, they alternate between a getaway of just a few days and a much longer trip to new locations around our country. I thoroughly enjoy these trips since there's always a riot of mirth, mischief, and mayhem, and I fit in quite well with this group of crazed family and friends. I've never yet heard of

6

anyone coming back from one of those trips and admitting they've actually learned anything, but we do see lots of our nation's beauty and we do sing well together. And we are so loud!

The bus trip planned for 2013 was one of longer duration, scheduled to travel west to Glacier National Park and Yellowstone National Park and then on up into Canada to Banff National Park. The 5,000-mile romp across the United States and Canada would take almost three weeks and was scheduled to depart several weeks before my own planned departure for the headwaters of the Mississippi in Lake Itasca, Minnesota.

I admit that 49 percent of me wanted to be on that bus. But the group would not return before I was scheduled to leave Ohio for Minnesota, so I would have to choose. The remaining 51 percent of me chose the river. Sadly, most of my brain had voted with the 49 percent minority.

But the final vote was swung by the knowledge that there are times when it does a person good to get out alone and contemplate in solitude. I'd learned this on all my other hikes and adventures, and this was what I hoped to find again as I paddled.

I *needed* to find this again.

So I had made a choice to forego the craziness of cousins, comforts of the bus, and warm nights in motels in order to endure unrelenting attacks by bugs, cold nights in a tent, and mile after mile of stinking swamps.

Planning my paddle, I had started, of course, with the necessity of buying a vessel. I did admire Huck Finn for building his own raft, but from the little research I had done, I realized something more substantial was needed.

My launch into learning about everything nautical became as confusing as my attempts to purchase the best gear for my hike on the Appalachian Trail had been; but I did read, with alarming clarity, the clues as to what I might encounter along my route. Giant waves produced by passing barges, submerged logs, difficult navigation through locks, dangerous currents, life-threatening lake weather, and unsavory characters were a few of the things I could expect to meet.

The more I researched, the better that bus trip sounded. Perhaps I should abandon the river and hop on the bus instead. But no, I didn't. It was New Orleans or bust!

I would need a kayak that could handle large waves. I perused eBay and sifted through hundreds of listings for used canoes and kayaks. A fellow out in Chicago had a used hybrid kayak/canoe that seemed to fit the bill. It was a Sea 1 Clipper, from Clipper Canoes, a Canadian company. The Clipper was billed as a sea-touring vessel; the owner in Chicago assured me it could ride over four-foot swells like a trouper. He had used it on Lake Michigan, and it had performed admirably.

The Sea 1 Clipper was 17' 9" long. Too long for all the tight corners I would encounter in the swamps—but then, I had no inkling of the maneuvering I'd be doing in those first days on the river. Built of lightweight Kevlar®, it weighed only 55 pounds and was supposedly tougher than fiberglass. A racing paddle was included. This instrument had a much shorter shaft than the usual kayak paddle and a single wide, long blade. I also purchased a two-bladed paddle, the standard type used in kayaking.

My new Sea 1 Clipper was neither kayak nor canoe, but a hybrid of the two. It sat higher than most kayaks do—more like a canoe in that feature—but was covered with a spray skirt, like a kayak. A spray skirt is exactly what the name implies. It's a protective cover that stretches across the cockpit and fits snugly around the paddler. I never did enclose myself totally in that cocoon. Suppose a water evacuation became necessary? Experienced kayakers can do a maneuver known as the barrel roll, in which the occupant of a kayak flips his kayak—putting himself head down, under water—and then continues through a 360-degree roll, uprighting the kayak and himself in seconds. If a wave hits and flips the dude, he just rolls around and pops back above water.

My limited expertise only allowed me to do half of that maneuver. In an emergency situation on a stormy sea, a 180-degree roll would have my head facing in entirely the wrong direction. I wanted that spray skirt loosened, just in case.

It was highly likely that I would get wet, sometime. Two "dry bags," designed to be airtight and waterproof, would protect my things, and I also stowed valuables in a bicycle pannier I had used on my cross-country bike ride. I hoped the pannier, too, was waterproof. It held my wallet, iPad, maps, and other things I did not wish to lose to the river.

I would need maps. My search turned up a source for the river maps used by barge captains navigating the Mississippi. These maps are detailed by river section and assembled in two spiral-bound books. I assumed they would be of a size suitable to tuck away in my dry bags, and I ordered a set. But when the package arrived, they were far too large and heavy to lug around. The Minnesota Department of Natural Resources produced small, segmented maps of the Minnesota portion of the river. I decided to start with those and worry about Iowa if and when I got there.

What else would be required? Experience? After one very short trial paddle on the Tuscarawas River and with the lingering memory of my peaceful trip through the Black Canyon, I thought I was ready to expertly guide my craft through whatever lay along the watery trail that was beckoning me. Granted, our little Tuscarawas is nothing like the Mississippi—except, water is water, right? The Mississippi would just be bigger, deeper, and longer, right?

About the time I was completely outfitted for the upcoming trip, another opportunity presented itself. I didn't give it much consideration. I had already turned down a cushy bus trip, and if I said yes to this new opportunity, it would mean I'd have to scrap the river trip, at least for another year.

My friend Ivan called one day and suggested we meet for lunch. He had recently been hired by a local company that had started as a small Amish business in an off-the-beaten path hamlet and had grown to be one of the county's largest, most successful enterprises. The owner, the man who had guided the company through this transformation, had been diagnosed with cancer several years before. His two sons were now part of the leadership at the company, and they had shared with Ivan their desire to preserve in book form the story of their parents' lives and the building of a successful business. At lunch that day, Ivan relayed their request: Would I undertake the task of writing the book?

I was not so insensitive that I missed the sense of urgency; I knew only too well how a cancer diagnosis changes one's perspective on everything. But I had made my plans. I gave the proposal consideration—for all of 30 seconds.

"That's not something anywhere on my radar, Ivan. You know I'm kayaking the Mississippi River this summer. And when I get back, I'll be writing my book about that adventure, so I need to pass on any other huge project for now."

Looking back, I see that of course I should have taken some time to contemplate the offer in dialogue with God, but I had already made my plans. Most of my summer was going to be spent kayaking, exploring the Mississippi from its headwaters to the Gulf of Mexico. As is so often the case in my life, I was running a few steps ahead of God and hoping He would catch up with me.

And, of course, He did. Very quickly.

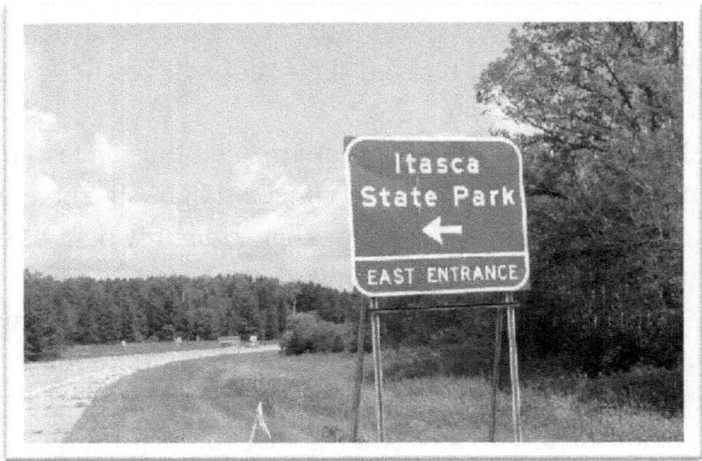

Chapter 3

In the parking lot of the Mary Gibbs Mississippi Headwaters Center at Itasca State Park, Ivan and I unloaded the kayak from atop his van. He and his wife, Fran, had brought me to Minnesota to give me a proper send-off. I installed wheels on the small kayak cart, and we positioned the Clipper on it, finding the center of balance. With the cart precisely placed, moving the almost-18-foot kayak became quite easy.

Before we exited the parking lot to start down the trail leading to the river, Ivan prayed for my safety. And then he startled me with this statement:

"Paul, you don't have to do this."

"What are you talking about?"

His reply was vague and troubling. He'd had a dream the previous night, portending some disaster that I would meet on the river.

"Exactly what kind of disaster?" I asked.

"You don't have to do it," he repeated.

I glanced at Fran. Here I was, ready to set sail. We'd just traveled 1,000 miles, and—well, we all knew I wasn't going to turn around and go home.

"Thanks for that bit of wisdom," I said, with more than a bit of sarcasm. I admit, though, I was a bit unsettled as we pulled the cart and kayak down a path toward the water.

And then I scoffed at my own fears as I waded out into the mighty Mississippi River and the water reached all the way up to my ankles. Whatever Ivan had seen foreshadowed in his dream, it could not have included my drowning—at least, not for the foreseeable future.

Early explorers had pronounced Cass Lake and the Turtle River, 50 miles east of Lake Itasca, as the headwaters of the Mississippi River. The Ojibwe tribes, though, insisted that the source was farther west, here, in this lake on the highest point in the region. In 1832, Henry Rowe Schoolcraft, an explorer and geographer, determined to find the headwaters that the Native Americans talked of, and he and his party followed an Ojibwe guide, Ozaawindib (Yellow Head), to the lake. Now that sounds like a simple enough expedition, does it not? But in less than nine days, I would have far more appreciation for what these folks went through in order to stand where I now stood, ankle-deep in the beginnings of the great Mississippi River.

As it begins its flow to the Gulf, the river leaves Lake Itasca over a low dam of stones placed there in the 1930s. My kayak was in the water, waiting. I got in—and promptly felt the ground under me. Apparently, this craft was quite reliable in four-foot waves on Lake Michigan, but it would quit on me in five inches of water.

I stepped out, pulled the kayak forward a bit, sat down again with my legs hanging over the sides, and wiggled, but there was just not enough water to float the kayak along. I got out again.

This is a historic, famous spot, and we were not alone. A number of folks were walking about, wading, stepping across the stones. Somehow the word got out: The man pulling his kayak down the river is heading to New Orleans, Louisiana. Shouts of encouragement followed me as I tugged my boat along. Here the river was about five feet wide and five inches deep. It was hard to imagine that this would ever turn into anything substantial.

After several hundred feet, I could sit in the kayak and actually float. Now we're moving! Then I ground to a stop again as the kayak bottomed out. After a few more starts and stops, I approached a low bridge. Scrunching down into the kayak, I was able to float beneath, then I waved goodbye to the assembly watching from above and, with a "See you in New Orleans," I paddled off into the unknown.

Ah, here was the placid scene of tranquility that I had envisioned. Low overhanging branches on my left and assorted unknown foliage on my right lined the river, about 12 feet wide here and with an entire inch of clearance beneath my boat. Several ducks floated in the water ahead of me. It really was quite a beautiful sight.

If these conditions continued, I could realize my goal of 15 miles this afternoon. I surmised that I had at least seven hours of daylight, and at a minimum of two to three miles an hour, I could reach a primitive camp area known as Coffee Pot Landing. My research showed a small wooden shelter there, similar to many places I had slept while hiking the Appalachian Trail.

But my calculations did not factor in everything I was about to encounter.

Before I could frighten the ducks into flight, my kayak ground to a stop again. Thus began a routine which became all too familiar over the next few days. Once again straddling the kayak, I pushed myself upright and wiggled my ride along until it was free of the rocks and sand. Occasionally, I exited the boat and pulled it along with the rope attached to the front end.

As I pushed deeper into the swamp, paddling was difficult. The tall swamp weeds rose above me, hiding me from view of any other creature. With the water level so low and the weeds so thick, I found it impossible to see enough movement of water to tell where the narrow channel was flowing. The channel actually spread out among the bulrushes and disappeared. Bumping and pushing along, I occasionally paused to cast a keen eye into the water, trying to discern even slight angles of the underwater foliage that might give me a hint of direction.

The grasses became ever denser until, finally, that one final thrust of my paddle told me there was no going forward. I was trapped. Stuck in the weeds.

This was *not* how the afternoon was supposed to flow. Grand and glorious visions of floating along the river were quickly draining away—disappearing faster than the Mississippi's waters—and self-pity and apprehension were beginning to move in on a quickly rising tide.

Mark Twain would never have found himself in such a predicament. He had actually worked on river barges and knew how to avoid waters that were too shallow. The barges required a certain clearance to avoid being grounded much like I was, and so a measuring rope hung overboard to check the depth of the Mississippi. This process was known as "marking twain"—and that's where Samuel Clemens acquired his pen name. Had I marked twain now, the rope might have measured one foot. Beneath that foot of murky water lay several feet of silt, muck, and mire.

I was deep in the swamp weeds. Literally, *deep.* They rose above me, blocking my view of my surroundings. I had no sense if I was anywhere near a place where I could possibly drag myself out of the swamp. I'd been using my graphite racing paddle to move myself along by paddling—not the water, but the weeds. The smaller paddle, though, was useless in loosening the swamp's clutches. I unlashed the larger kayak paddle, normally used in deeper, open water.

This paddle now would have to serve as a pole. I angled it as far as possible into the muddy bottom. Putting my weight into the improvised pole, I pushed with all my might and slowly backed away from the tangled grasses. Then with feverish swirls of the paddle, I mowed down swamp foliage left and right, trying to locate any small trench with enough water to float the kayak. Moving slightly to the left, I found only more miserable grass and no flow. More swamp grass destruction ensued. Then I spotted what looked like a narrow 2-foot channel about 15 feet to my right. Paddling the weeds ferociously, I inched my kayak toward that small hope.

I saw that I was once again back on my mighty Mississippi River, and the sigh of relief that exploded from me frightened several thousand small frogs.

Still, I battled these conditions for the next few hours. At times, the flow widened or the weeds thinned enough that the underwater foliage pointed me in the right direction.

Steering the kayak was also a problem. There was a rudder attached to the kayak; the pull of a rope situated to the right of my seat would flip the rudder downward, and foot pedals in the cockpit gave me further control of direction. The rudder was useless here. It would get caught on swamp grasses and would, in essence, be no more than a swamp plow.

Sharp hairpin turns challenged all my navigational skills. Over the next few days, I learned that all I could do on the sharp turns was to go straight into the bank ahead of me, then reverse the kayak by paddling backward, and proceed to wiggle my way around the bends.

After fighting my way through the weeds for hours, I was relieved when the river widened a bit and I spotted a bridge in the distance. Surely I was nearing my destination of Coffee Pot Landing. I paddled beneath the bridge and drifted to shore. After the hours of struggles, starts, and stops, I estimated I had covered at least eight miles of the fifteen to Coffee Pot. I located the landing on the map. The area was Gulsvig Landing, a small parcel of land donated by a local family to give folks access to the river at this point. Minnesota Highway 200 passed across the small bridge looming overhead.

Wait... Was this map in error? I sat in the weeds along the bank and stared at the map in great dismay. It showed that I had only traversed two miles. At this rate, I would never reach Coffee Pot this day. At this rate, I wouldn't even reach New Orleans this year. I had planned to be done with this paddle in less than three months. Unless I picked up the pace, I would witness all four seasons on the Mississippi.

Wanagan Landing lay another three miles ahead. The map promised a camping spot set among spruce trees. I adjusted my goals and hoped to reach that before nightfall.

Once again, the river narrowed, and once again, I was forced to battle through areas choked with weeds and only occasional open channels.

After another frightening and challenging three miles, I knew I was a prisoner of this swamp. Dusk was settling, and I felt great relief when I came around a sharp bend and spotted a small, three-sided log shelter surrounded by spruce trees up on a grassy overlook.

No Hilton or Sheraton had ever looked better.

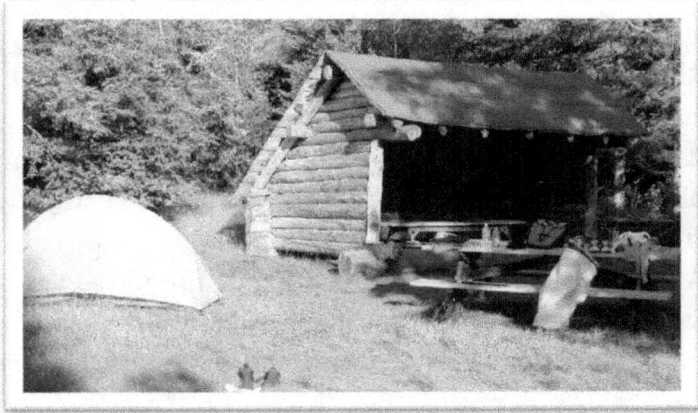

Chapter 4

Extricating myself from the swamp's clutches, I grounded my kayak against the river bank. I stepped out, sank into the muck, and slogged to dry ground, pulling the kayak out of the river and up onto the grass. My boat was covered with mud and swamp weeds.

Back in Chicago, while loading my newly purchased kayak, I had asked the previous owner if he had a bilge pump.

"Sure do, and I won't even charge you," he had said.

With that, he reached up to a shelf and tossed a dirty sponge my way.

"That's the only thing I've ever used."

The sponge had come in handy earlier in the day when all of my flailing about in the swamp weeds had thrown water into the cockpit. And it did work quite well. I now used it to give the boat a quick sponge bath with the dirty swamp water.

All my camping gear, cooking equipment, clothes, and food were stored in the two dry bags. One bag was stowed up in front of the kayak, and the other in the cavity behind my seat. Grabbing both dry bags now, I set off to see if there was a vacancy at the shelter.

A picnic table was positioned in the middle of the shelter on bare ground. The interior of the structure reeked of rotting fish and was littered with refuse and detritus from previous occupants. Apparently, the "leave no trace" mantra so common in the hiking community did not apply here. Spending a night inside would not be a pleasant experience.

I had brought all my camping gear with me, and I realized I was actually looking forward to spending a night in the tent. The last time I had erected that tent was the night before I finished my hike on the Appalachian Trail. I had reserved a cabin at the base of Mt. Katahdin, but still I erected the tent inside the cabin so that I could spend the last night of my hike within its shelter. That had been August 12, 2008. This day was August 12, 2013. Tomorrow, it would be five years since the hike that changed my life had ended on the top of that mountain in Maine.

I quickly set up my tent—outside the shelter—as the evening shadows crept across the landscape.

I'd also brought the last packages of dehydrated meals left from my hike. The expiration date on the package was 2013.

It's amazing how long food can be stored when deprived of life-sustaining water. I went about reconstituting my five-year-old grub, pulling out the water filter that had always provided me with clean water in the Appalachian wilderness.

The filter would now be put to its most difficult test. When I purchased that filter, the sales person informed me it was one of the best on the market. Using this, you could make any filthy water potable, he had promised. At the river bank, I dropped the intake tube into the swamp water and—as soon as the dastardly snake slithered away—started the process of changing putrid water into a drinkable beverage.

That transformation took a good bit of effort. When I was finished, I had to completely disassemble and clean the charcoal filter, which was now clogged with swamp muck.

Spaghetti was the main course that evening, and I recalled how rewarding a warm meal had been at the end of a long day of hiking. Whether on a hike, bike ride, or river paddle, my needs were simple—food, clothing, and shelter.

The sun slipped down over the farthest edge of the vast swamp and wisps of fog drifted in. Soon the entire swampy bottom was covered with a soft blanket of fog, as though Night was tucking in the world for a restful sleep.

Before retiring myself, I checked my phone. No service. Just as I'd suspected. I was alone, completely alone, and I felt the isolation so acutely.

Why do I do this?

Inside the tent, I slipped into my 45-degree sleeping bag. I wished I had brought my 5-degree bag instead. My notion that August in Minnesota would be hot was yet another erroneous assumption. As in the western deserts I had pedaled through, these days were hot but nighttime brought an unexpected cold.

Complete darkness enveloped my camping area, and around me a cacophony of sounds rose from the swamp. Croaks of all timbres produced a symphony of nature. Off In the distance, coyotes howled back and forth. Perhaps it was wolves, I wasn't sure. The sounds were eerie and seemed to be coming closer. Every now and then I heard a car far off in the distance. Sleeping in starts and stops, I'd always wake to the sounds of nature's choir, with the voices changing during the night.

It was not the choir that kept waking me, however. It's hard to sleep when your body is shivering violently. I'd wake, light my propane cook stove until the tent warmed up a bit, and then fall asleep—until the cold again became intolerable. Then I'd wake. Light the stove. Fall asleep. Shiver.

The inexorably long night finally ended, and I hoped to get an early start on my slog through the quagmire. It was not to be. The evening's enchanting mist had mutated during the night, mingling and coalescing with fog and swamp waters to become a maelstrom of moisture that socked in the entire area and locked me into zero visibility. It wasn't raining, but it sure looked and felt like the fog was crying. Perhaps it was a harbinger of what lay ahead.

I waited in my tent. It was the only thing I could do.

By eight o'clock, the fog had lifted enough that I felt I could go outside and explore my surroundings. I normally do this upon arrival at a campsite, but I had been so totally exhausted the previous evening that just setting up camp, filtering water, and making dinner was all I could manage. I went for a short walk, and, around a corner, found a clearing where I spied a pump handle. The handle was even attached to a pump. I was exasperated to think how much effort I had put into filtering swamp water when fresh water was nearby. There was also a path that led to an outhouse. I had no idea my camp had such amenities. The discovery was a relief—in many ways.

As soon as the morning sun had burned off enough fog that I could navigate, I broke camp and shoved off into the wild.

Today had to be better. How could things possibly get worse?

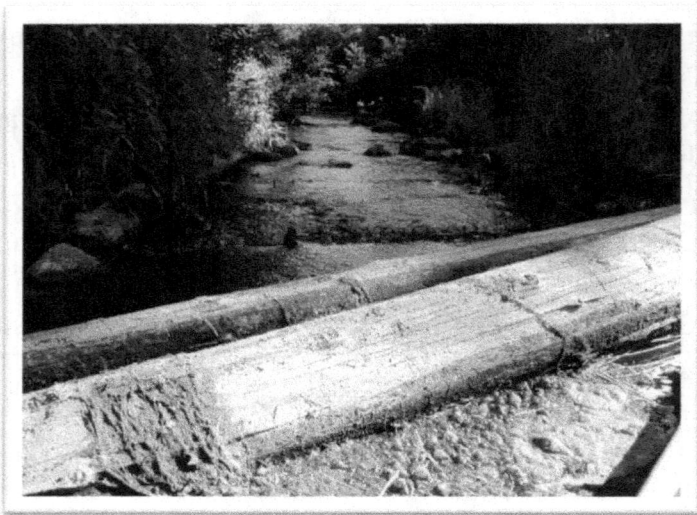

Chapter 5

Several weeks before leaving for Minnesota, I had purchased a book written by Jim Lewis, who lives by the river in a small town named Cohasset. He had led a group of men down the Mississippi River in trips over several years. The book detailed their travails floundering through the section of wetlands I was about to enter. They, however, had the assistance of a GPS in finding the channel of the river. Even with that technological aid, they sometimes found themselves stuck and disoriented. I had read the book. I should have been prepared for this day. I should have realized the fog was shedding tears that morning for this solitary traveler.

I was learning to read the river. Wooded areas lay at the edges of the wetlands. There, between the swamp grasses and the woods, I often found deeper, clearer water. But there was a price to pay for navigational clarity. Those passages often had downed trees, either lying under water, waiting to grab my kayak, or boldly blocking the waterway to thwart all passage. After a few miles, the river turned toward the weeds again, and my struggle against the clutches of the swamp continued.

I had simply exchanged one misery for another.

One stretch of river flowed through a spruce forest where logging had taken place many years before. Early in the twentieth century, a wooden dam had been built across the river to facilitate the floating of logs downriver. The dam was a simple terraced series of logs over which I could have stepped, but it blocked the forward progress of my kayak. My map showed a pathway through the woods, and suggested that a person would need to portage around this obstruction.

But a portage would mean beaching my craft, making several trips carrying my dry bags to the next point of entry into the river, then stumbling through the woods with that nearly 18-foot appendage balanced on my shoulder. I could have, of course, assembled the kayak cart and tried to drag kayak and contents over rocks and roots in one bumpy trip, but who knew what kind of path there was through the woods? Would it even be possible to use the cart?

In the end, it seemed easier to just drag the kayak and contents over the log dam.

The water pushed up against the top log but was not flowing over it. Instead, it seeped and trickled around and beneath the log. Green river slime sloshed around me as I navigated as close to the log as I could. The current swung the kayak sideways, pinning it against the log, and I could see beyond this first obstacle to the terraced rows of logs placed about 10 feet apart.

It would work, I thought. At least, it was worth a try. With the kayak still hugging the top of the dam, I braced one arm on the log and gingerly rolled my body out of the kayak, across the log, and into the water on the other side. Grabbing the rope at the front of the kayak, I tugged and coaxed my craft across the first log. Success! Section by section, I led my boat, bumping and bouncing, over each log until I reached the bottom of the dam.

I straddled the kayak and dropped down onto the seat. Oh, what a sweet triumph! Who needs to portage?

According to the map, the next four miles promised some excitement: an abundance of rocks and sandbars created a series of Class I rapids. Class I rapids are the lowest class, small, usually posing very little danger, just a section where the current runs a little faster with a few bumps along the way.

Still full of exhilaration at my defeat of the log dam, I welcomed these rapids—it meant I could make better time. I had set an aggressive goal for this day. By evening, I wanted to be at Fox Trap campsite, 25 miles away. These rapids would speed me on my way.

As with everything else thus far, I had miscalculated.

Not one little riffle appeared. The rocks that should have been submerged, creating my hoped-for rapids, were plainly visible. The promised four-mile run ended before it even began. My kayak came to a grinding halt in the low water, and the next four miles saw me—instead of bobbing merrily on my way—splashing through the water, dragging the kayak along. At some places, I even had to pick up that seaworthy Clipper and lift it over the rocks.

At last I reached a bridge. The map declared this to be County Road 2 crossing the river. Just beyond the bridge, the river reentered the wetlands. I breathed a sigh of relief and hoped my kayak would soon be transporting me down the river again, instead of me having to do all the work of moving forward.

Of course, this hope was not to be realized.

I entered an area where the water mysteriously deepened a bit. Before I even had a chance to rejoice at this development, I rounded a hairpin curve and saw the cause of the deeper water—a beaver dam. I was paddling down Beaver Avenue in Beavertown. My map noted a series of these river obstacles ahead of me. But how does one portage around beaver dams when swamps lie on all sides?

I had gone over top of the log dam; why not just rudely go over top of the beavers' lodging?

I approached the beaver jam-up and studied the jumbled pile of gnawed branches. As I did with the previous dam, I slid my kayak up against the wall and tested the firmness of the construction. It was a bit spongy, but I judged that it could take my weight. There was a bit of crackling and snapping as I crawled over and then dragged the kayak across. I stood in knee deep water as the kayak landed back in the river. Mr. Beaver would need to repair a few roof trusses, but otherwise I left the construction in good shape.

In the next few hours, I became quite adept at crossing beaver dams. Some were like a two-story house and more manipulation was required to cross these than the one-story ranches. The low-rise dams actually presented a new challenge: they sat so low in the water that I thought I could probably cross them without exiting my kayak. A good burst of speed produced by frantic paddling usually slid the kayak over. If a burst of speed was not adequate propulsion and the kayak didn't quite make it across, I'd sit in my cockpit and perform some highly technical wiggling and rocking until we were free and once again waterborne.

More side channels confused navigation. Some of them were completely dried out—at least, I knew those were dead ends. I kept an eye on my underwater guidance system (UGS). Just a slight movement of the weeds in the water directed me forward. But the taller weeds towering above me again grew thicker, and some places grew so dense that it was impossible to detect any current at all.

Once again, the weeds stopped me. Forward movement was impossible. I know it's hard to imagine, but those weeds held me so tightly that I feared my graphite paddle would break from the force I was applying as I tried to push myself into reverse.

It was time to bring out the big gun again. The kayak paddle had been useful as a pole. Now it became a scythe. I thrashed about, mowing down weeds left and right. Then, submerging the paddle deep in the mud, I pushed back with all my strength. Slowly the grasses released their grip. I pushed to the left and was immediately stuck again. More flailing and thrashing served to clear another patch of swamp. At last I glimpsed a two-foot sliver of water to my right and poled in a tight circle toward freedom. Anyone flying overhead that day witnessed mysterious swamp circles appearing out in the wetlands of Minnesota.

Never had I expected to be using this paddle as a pole or a harvester of swamp grass. No, I had other expectations of this long, two-bladed instrument.

My previous kayaking experience amounted to two and a half trips: One experience was more of a "float" through the mangrove forest in Florida, one trip was in Black Canyon, and the "half" was a brief splashing in the Tuscarawas River. On those occasions, the conditions had been far superior to this trip—more water, no obstructions, and cooperative currents that did most of the work for me. My paddling technique in those experiences had consisted of gripping the paddle however I could and furiously splashing it about in the water. It was exciting but tiring—and not overly effective.

As I'd prepared for this trip, I did do some research on proper techniques of paddling. After all, I was going to be on the river several months. Watching tutorials that showed the proper way of holding the paddle and how to precisely, silently, and effortlessly slip it into the water with barely a splash, I had visions of developing a powerful stroke that shot me forward. Just a slight twist of the wrist, and the paddle blade angles out of the water with ease.

What really impressed me was that proper paddling form required use of the stomach muscles—not the shoulder and arm muscles that I'd been overworking in Florida and on the Colorado. The stomach muscles are used to force the blade through the water. That eliminates shoulder soreness.

I couldn't wait to try this new method, and I admit to some vanity coming into play here. I would achieve this perfect stroke, and after paddling over 2,000 miles, I'd re-enter my social world with rippling chest muscles and a six-pack torso. The cost of a new wardrobe would simply be the price for looking good, because surely my old shirts would rip apart trying to cover this newly toned body.

As you already know, I was wrong about a lot of things.

Now, the only result of poling, pushing, and mowing weeds was extremely sore shoulder muscles. The arm muscles were perhaps tightening a bit, but the stomach muscles weren't getting into the game at all.

Once again, the swamp pushed me out, closer to the edge of the wetlands and the surrounding woods. Occasionally I reached the breathtaking speed of close to one mile per hour. I adjusted my goal. Fox Trap Camp would be tomorrow's stop. But I did want to reach Coffee Pot yet today. Off in the distance, I saw a bridge. Clearwater County Road 40 crossed here. And as I neared the bridge, I heard voices.

Understand, I had heard nothing more than swamp croakings for more than two days. I floated beneath the bridge and toward the bank, in search of bodies attached to the voices. Beaching my craft, I stepped out onto the bank and sank in mud up to my knees. Retreating back into the water, I tried to wash off the mud.

A man and woman appeared on the bridge above me and were shocked to see a human being in the river.

"Didn't expect to see anyone here," they said.

Those were my sentiments as well, but I was delighted to find people. The couple lived in Grand Rapids, Minnesota, and they were out for an evening ride. They'd stopped at the small parking area next to the bridge.

"Not many folks come through here with the river so low," they offered. I could understand why.

"Where's Coffee Pot Landing?" I asked.

"You're there. The shelter is back above the bridge, on the right."

I had been so intent on avoiding a rock protruding from the river and finding people to talk with that I had missed my stop.

"Those rocks are usually under water. I can't imagine that the river's even navigable right now."

"It really isn't," I said.

They pointed out a river level gauge. These gauges are posted at many points along the river. Some are wooden posts; some are painted on bridge abutments. They simply mark the height of the river to assist travelers in knowing whether or not the area is navigable. My map explained that if the river here was over three feet, the water was high. The average was between 1.9 and 3.5 feet. Below 1.9 feet was "shallow." On this day, the gauge registered one foot. I knew then that the next day would bring more headaches, heartaches, turmoil, and trouble.

I dragged the kayak back upstream and located the pullout site. The shelter sat back from the river and was accessible from the road. It also showed considerable wear and was in even worse condition than the one I'd stayed at the previous night. A young couple with two kids wandered over while I pitched my tent. They listened to my tales of travail and attempted to explain to the small children the task I had undertaken. The children were more interested in watching the tent go up.

At last I had the area to myself. I faced another long cold night. Alone again, with no phone service. At least there was a road nearby. But as I settled in, I realized that whether on the AT or out here in the swamp, I actually preferred more distance between my camp and any road. Isolation somehow felt safer.

Exchanging words and thoughts with other humans had been wonderful, though. The couple from Grand Rapids had even offered me transportation to a camp site and an invitation to a meal when I reached their town.

While the swamp choir worked up to a crescendo pitch, I lay shivering in my sleeping bag and reflected on the day's challenges. Five years ago, to this very day, I had achieved a lifetime goal when I completed my hike on the AT. After that last grueling climb up Mt. Katahdin, I thought I would probably never again be challenged both mentally and physically to the extent that the AT hike had pushed me. Of course, five years ago I would never have imagined that I'd be in the swamps of the upper Mississippi, fighting all they had in store for me.

I did hope the worst was behind me.

Chapter 6

It was another night of croaks from the river, howls from the nearby woods, and unceasing shivers inside my tent. Lighting my cook stove numerous times kept me thawed but gave me a splitting headache.

Morning mercifully arrived, and I once again had to wait for the fog to lift before I could continue on my way. By 9 a.m., visibility was good enough to join the swamp critters.

The map warned of a large wetland area for the next four miles and possible difficulty finding the channel if the water was low. I plowed back into the swamp. Twists and turns took me deep into the maze. False channels and dead ends frustrated my progress. Again, the current flow was so minimal that even my UGS was often useless. An occasional beaver dam deepened the water and made paddling easier for a short stretch, but then it was always up and over the building complex.

After four painstakingly slow miles, I entered a two-mile channel lined with spruce trees on the left bank. Again, the map said this was a stretch of rapids, but I splashed through the river dragging my ride over sandbars and around rocks. For a few short distances, I could sit and float—until a grating sound accompanied a sudden stop, and I was firmly grounded on another rock.

Another five-mile stretch of wetland. Another warning that if the water was low, finding the channel could be difficult. I had just started into this section when I was confronted with a large tree blocking the river. Branches, leaves, and other detritus had piled up against and on top of it. Apparently, there were actually times when the water was higher.

All of those beaver dams had been conquered, so a large tree should be no problem. I'd use the same strategy. It had worked well thus far.

I was forgetting, though, that beaver dams and large tree trunks are not constructed in the same way. The beavers build with twigs and small logs that fit together loosely and are somewhat pliant. A tree, though surrounded also with twigs and branches, is a rigid, unyielding surface.

I climbed onto the log and pulled the kayak up to rest beside me. The log sat low enough in the water that I judged this to be similar to a ranch-level beaver dam; I should be able to get back into the kayak, scoot my craft and myself across the log, and slide smoothly into the water on the other side.

On most clear-thinking days I would have detected the defect in this plan. This was not a usual day, and my brain was not functioning at a level much higher than the brains of the thousands of tiny frogs on the banks.

The small hitch in this plan was that my boat had a keel at the back end. As I had slid over the beaver dams, the keel simply wiggled its way through that loose construction. The surface of this log, though, would not give a fraction of an inch. But I was not thinking of all those little details of kayak construction as I pulled my Clipper three-quarters of the way across. The front end of the kayak was in the water, the last quarter of the boat was resting high on the log. All I needed to do was scoot a foot or two forward.

I imagine all the frogs, ducks, and the myriad swamp insects keeled over with amazement and laughter as I keeled over. In a flash, the kayak flipped and I was in the water. Fear rushed to the surface first, then frustration, then anger. The sum of all the emotions was total shock. I couldn't believe I'd just shipwrecked.

I emerged from the depth of the miry pit—that is, I got my feet under me and stood up; the water was about chest high— and surveyed the scene. My kayak bobbed upside down, a few feet away. The pannier I had stowed beneath my seat was floating nearby. I hoped it was indeed waterproof; my iPad, wallet, and other valuables were within.

I uprighted the kayak, now filled with water. Amazing. Even with a good amount of water in it, it still rode above the water line. I had made my own bilge pump as I prepared for the trip, buying something similar to a bicycle tire pump at the hardware store and attaching plastic tubing. I rummaged in the back storage area of the Clipper and brought out the pump and started pumping. I was still standing in the river.

While I pumped away, I spotted my expensive foam seat cover floating downstream. It was already out of reach, but I hoped it would get snagged somewhere so that I'd eventually catch up to it and could retrieve it. The seat on the kayak was wooden and very uncomfortable without that foam cushion.

An hour later—an hour during which I stood in chest high water—I had pumped all the river out of the kayak and used the sponge to clean up my ride. I finally plopped back onto the hard seat and set off in pursuit of the seat cover. And then I remembered—my cell phone and camera had been in the pockets of my life jacket all this time. The camera had been borrowed from a friend. [Author's note: Do not ever loan me a camera of any sort, no matter how much I beg.]

I pulled them out. The camera now showed an eerie blue screen, and water leaked out of several joints and openings. My new iPhone was also dripping river, and its screen displayed an ominous red lightning bolt. I could not imagine that being a good sign.

In my concern for camera and phone, I forgot all about my seat cover and never saw it again. It may have finished the journey to New Orleans.

Letting the kayak float, I shook water from both instruments and laid them out on the open deck, hoping the sunlight would bake the moisture out of them.

Life had about bottomed out. I was alone in vast wetlands without phone or camera.

That five-mile stretch was just as difficult as the map had promised. Finally, another bridge appeared. I was in Beltrami County and this was County Road 5.

This time I looked for the river gauge. I wanted to know what travel conditions were ahead. The map stated that in this section of the river, "normal" was 6' to 7'6" of water, less than 6 feet was considered low, and less than 4 feet—well, then the river was not navigable. The gauge registered under 3 feet. The guiding map suggested a portage down a nearby forest road that would take me to Bear Den Landing and cut off over three miles of unnavigable wetlands.

Dragging through the forest would certainly have been easier, but I was determined to kayak the entire Mississippi River. I had thru-hiked the Appalachian Trail as a purist, passing every white blaze along the way. I had pedaled my bicycle nearly 5,000 miles from corner to corner of America without accepting a ride. What some folks might call stubborn and foolish, I call tenacious and undaunted. My dad's words often ring in my mind: *Son, whatever you do, do with your might. Things done by half are never done right.* He is a stickler for details. Another one of his favorite dictates is *Always buy quality*. If you buy quality equipment, you don't have to pay twice. I had purchased a good bicycle that gave me no mechanical problems and now had a boat of the highest quality.

This stretch was the last four miles to Fox Trap, a shelter accessible only by river travel. I could not imagine meeting any obstacles that would be more challenging than what I'd already battled. I plunged ahead.

The few feet of water at the bridge dwindled away to less than one foot in the swamp. The river twisted around one hairpin turn after another. The sun was hot overhead as I plowed my way toward day's end.

Since the rudder was useless here, I was still paddling with the racing paddle. I fell into a rhythm that kept the kayak on track. Paddling on the left side for a few strokes turned the front of the boat in one direction, then switching to the right side for a few strokes straightened it out again. Left, left, left. Right, right, right. I was certainly looking forward to deeper water where I could experiment with the rudder.

As paddling became more rhythmic, I added another movement—slap, slap, slap. The nasty swamp flies found my thighs attractive, and I soon had a growing collection of dead and dying insects on the floor of the kayak.

There were moments of inspiration. On one bank, a mama duck guarded her small ducklings and raised a hysterical alarm when she saw the swamp apparition approaching. After hustling them farther up the bank, she made quite a ruckus with her flapping about, trying to lead me away from her brood. As I approached a turn, two deer stood in the shallow stream. Their noses were in the water when I caught sight of them, but they saw me, too, and splashed off into the swamp. And I watched in wonderment as an eagle glided silently above me.

This was part of what I had come for—not whacking swamp weeds and poling mud. I reminded myself to be more watchful for these scenes.

Fox Trap was a small camping area nestled up on a rise overlooking the vast swamp.

I was the only inhabitant there, and there was no evidence of any other recent visitors. I dragged the canoe out of the stream and admired the variety of grasses and weeds, insects, and dirt covering it. I had quite a variety of specimens.

Physically and mentally exhausted, I carried the dry bags and supplies up the slope to the campsite. Water still dripped from everything as I plodded uphill.

In the rustic shelter, I unpacked my belongings. The dry bags had done well. The pannier had not. My journals and other papers were soaked. I spread everything out on a picnic table to dry overnight. The phone and camera were dead. I remembered reading somewhere that a wet phone could possibly be resurrected by submerging it in a bag of rice. The rice extracts the moisture from the phone. I had no rice, but I did have my dehydrated meals. I took a plastic bag and dumped two meals into it, then added the phone and camera, sealed the bag, and hoped for the best.

Since my iPad was the only instrument of modern technology left, I took a photo of the swamp from the direction I had come and a photo off into the direction I would go tomorrow.

As I gazed out into tomorrow, I visualized the trip getting easier. I was now 24 miles from the town of Bemidji. I had done nearly 16 miles on this extremely difficult day. It had to get easier. I could not imagine how this river could get still more difficult.

Sleep again came only in fits and starts. Sleep a bit, freeze, light the stove for warmth, sleep, freeze, repeat all night. The night filled with the cacophony of sounds rising from the swamp—and new sounds from the nearby woods. The rustling coming from the utter darkness of the trees was a bit frightening. There was no road nearby, so whatever was out there was no human. If Big Foot does exist, he may live in the woods near Fox Trap Shelter.

Chapter 7

Remember hell? I do.

That is to say, those of us who grew up in the Conservative Mennonite tradition do remember. Perhaps you, too, were raised in a church setting where the destination for the damned was preached with fervor. These days, folks seem to think that actual sins are more and more difficult to identify and define, and the need for hellfire and brimstone preaching has diminished. As sin has become less defined, our need for a savior also becomes more difficult to understand and accept.

But even when things in my world did seem much more black or white, right or wrong, good or evil, godly or sinful, I struggled with the idea of inviting Jesus into my heart to take away my sins. Sins? What sins? We were young, we followed church rules and obeyed our parents; yet we were told that unless we were saved, we were headed to hell.

I did, however, beg Jesus to take up residence—however that happened and in whatever heart chamber. Yet nothing changed. Where was that euphoria I should have been feeling? Other heinous sinners wept at the altar when they received their hell insurance. Sometimes I wondered if my salvation might not have "taken."

Repentance means a change of direction. You turn from a life of sin to a life of following Christ. But what does that mean exactly? I struggled with that for many years. For many of us, changing direction in life would have meant we needed to start sinning. We were "good" kids.

In the ensuing years, I have found that others raised in similar settings also struggle with the meaning of "accepting Jesus into your heart."

But there was one thing we all knew too well. There was no question about this. It was very clear—hell was to be avoided at all costs. So although I struggled to understand what it meant to follow Christ, I knew one thing: whatever it took, I did not want to go to hell.

But following Christ? It would take a lifetime of pilgrimage and a pilgrimage of a lifetime for me to discover what that really means.

Had there been a sign posted in the murky mire, it would have read, "Abandon all hope, ye who enter here." You might recognize that dire warning from a poem written on Good Friday in the year 1300. A middle-aged Italian named Dante Alighieri wrote a poem called "Divine Comedy." We know it better as Dante's Inferno. *Inferno* is the Italian name for hell.

Dante was lost in the woods while contemplating his life. He was being stalked by three creatures. Afraid and unsure how to find the right path to freedom, he followed a spirit who offered to guide him. However, the pathway to his freedom led through hell, depicted as having nine concentric circles. That is, circles within circles, leading ever deeper into the earth until at last reaching circle nine at the center of the earth—where the devil himself resided.

Travelers entering the first circle were greeted by the now famous sign: "Abandon all hope, ye who enter here. "

The circles represented sins such as lust, greed, gluttony, and violence. Lost souls were imprisoned in the circle of whatever sin had doomed them to this place.

The fifth circle was for anger, holding wrathful sinners in a swampy area created by the river Styx. Some folks were fighting each other in the muck and mire while others lay in the marsh. Gurgling noises emanated from the quagmire. Someone with a skiff arrived and transported Dante across this horror to circle number six, heresy.

The best lessons in life are lessons learned while living life. Just in case I'd forgotten about the torment and misery of hell as preached in my youth, I was about to be given another message on hell—in living color.

On my fourth day in the swamp, I entered the fifth circle of hell.

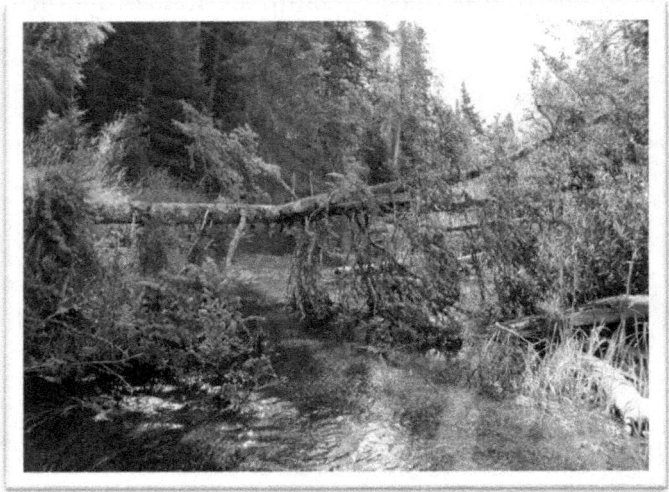

Chapter 8

My hope for this fourth day was to paddle through the swamp and all the way to Bemidji, Minnesota. It would be a 24-mile marathon, since there were no camping areas listed on my map for that entire stretch. And besides, I desperately needed to be in touch with civilization once again.

The long day would require an early start, and I was cheered to see the morning fog burn off early. I wondered if this could possibly be the day that my river traveling finally became easier.

The map stated that I was again entering large wetlands. (*Entering*? I didn't realize I'd ever left.) It further described the river meandering through said wetlands until reaching an area called Iron Bridge, about eight miles distant.

Wetlands. Meandering. It all sounded so calm and soothing. I'd just float along, meandering among the fauna and foliage. Life is but a dream.

Descriptive words can certainly distort reality. I was in a stinking swamp, and the river didn't meander—it was a circuitous, tortuous maze of eternal captivity in a miserable bog. But first, see that cute fawn by the river bank. Oh yes, those ducks are neat. The thousand little frogs scampering up the banks sure have their work cut out for them. If the water was higher, it would make life easier for all of us.

Excessive vegetation may make this area impassible. So said whoever published my little map. Were they unaware of the miles of excessive vegetation I had already plowed through?

Unfortunately, the pathway to hell wasn't paved with good intentions; instead it was clogged with all this excessive vegetation. I did plow along Vegetation Boulevard for several hours, with frequent stops caused by the meeting and greeting of rock tops and kayak bottom.

Then the water mysteriously deepened a bit, and I wondered if I might actually be out of the weeds. At once my kayak came to a stop. This was not the grinding stop I was used to. It was as if some silent monster had reached out of the pit and grabbed my ride. I glanced starboard. (Or was it port?) My head might have done a complete 360-degree swivel, seeking the cause of my newest predicament.

Something akin to a walrus or manatee or perhaps even a hippo had latched onto my craft.

I had been warned by the map, of course. This meandering wetland—nay, this stinking swamp—was actually a bog. Many dead, decaying plants, trees, insects, birds, animals, and possibly even a few river paddlers like me had been turned into peat over the eons of time. When conditions were right, large chunks of this bog separated and drifted about. This, of course, made finding the channel even more difficult. It's very disconcerting to find that what you think is "land" is constantly shifting and moving about. Some of these bog chunks float underwater, making progress difficult. My map again finessed the words a bit calling it all *a potential navigational hazard*.

I rested on my chunk of bog, feeling much like Noah's ark atop Mount Ararat, and surveyed the landscape. With cautious prodding of my paddle and tentative lurching of my body, I managed to slide the kayak off the mountain of decay.

For seven miles, I did meander. Round and round I meandered. Pick a channel, any channel. All channels lead somewhere. Most lead back to where you started. The swamp was mocking me. Yes, there is one channel that will lead you to where you want to go, but few there are who find it.

For the next few hours, I strained to see even the slightest movement of current. Frustration was nearing a fever pitch. I did develop a skilled eye for detecting dark spots on the river ahead where just the top of a floating bog waited. An occasional log lurking beneath the surface would abruptly bounce my boat from side to side.

Am I doomed to be in this swamp forever? I'm in hell! This must be what it's like. Forever stuck, going in circles, never getting out. Abandon all hope, ye swamp travelers.

At last I meandered my way out of that fifth circle of swamp maze, bog-shocked and weary. Nothing, I imagined, could be more terrible. Surely now I would have an easier go of it.

When I finally emerged from the primordial ooze, I drifted up against the near bank and heaved great sighs of relief. My ride was in much need of a washing, with a plethora of swamp grasses littering the deck and floor.

Hoping for the best, I checked the map once again to see what nature had in store for me next. Once again, it sounded lovely and serene: *The river enters a deeply wooded floodplain forest, where elm and cottonwood arch overhead.*

A closer reading revealed fine print that stated, *Numerous log jams exist in this section.* Well, how difficult could this be? I'd already overcome a log dam, beaver dams, submerged logs, floating bogs, bugs, getting stuck in the weeds, a trip to Davey Jones Locker—and all of that didn't even begin to match the loneliness I was feeling. What's two miles of log jams?

Around the river bend, the difficulty came into view. Sure, many of those elm and cottonwood trees did indeed arch overhead. However, hundreds more had arched themselves into the river, blocking my advance.

If you understand the concept of the child's game known as pick-up-sticks, you can visualize what awaited me. It was as if some giant had taken a vast handful of trees and dropped them hither and yon, creating a jumble of logs and branches.

Why, oh why, wouldn't someone clean up this mess? There are places in America where logging companies send divers to river bottoms scavenging for logs. This was not one of those rivers. Hundreds of thousands of board feet of lumber were strewn about, just waiting for some enterprising person. I suspected some arcane government rule may have prohibited that from happening. Perhaps the locals wanted it that way, preferring to deter traffic through this area. Locals—what locals? I hadn't seen a building in four days.

Slowly I maneuvered my way through this newest maze. Where the river depth allowed, the kayak lifted over obstructing logs. More dangerous logs lay just beneath the water surface, scraping my boat as I lurched across. Bending low, I slipped beneath the grasping limbs of others.

The current that I had so desperately searched for earlier now made it presence known—and it was not my friend. It pushed and pinned my kayak against the logs. I had purchased a machete with a sharpened blade on one side and a sawtooth blade on the other. When the thicket of trees clogging the river made passage impossible, I sawed my way through branches and inched along.

Finally, I cleared the last web of twisted branches and logs and reached navigable water. In the distance appeared a mirage of sorts—or was that actually a house?

Yes, it *was* a house, with a lawn and fields stretching outwards. I had survived the bog, I had meandered my way through the swamps, and I had squirmed through the log impasse. I hoped—oh, how I hoped!—that respite in a town inhabited *by people* lay ahead.

Chapter 9

For an experienced kayaker, a one-mile lake crossing is no big deal. For me, however, who had never been farther than swimming distance from shore, it summoned a great deal of apprehension.

As I neared Bemidji, the river widened and deepened. Lake Irving lay between me and the comfort of a motel room and food. I could see buildings in the distance. I could also see the lake that must be crossed. My map warned me to stay in the river channel which ran through the heart of Lake Irving, since there are submerged pilings where the channel crosses beneath a bridge leading to Bemidji. On the other side of the bridge, the Mississippi enters Lake Bemidji and crosses it in a three-mile channel.

Fortunately, Lake Irving seemed placid, and I tentatively started across. It was time to retire my shorter, one-bladed paddle and bring out the big gun. The two-bladed paddle (which I was counting on to give me a Charlie Atlas body) had so far been useful only in extricating myself from bog stumps and weeds.

I could also now use my rudder. Grasping the rope at my side, I gave it a tug and the rudder flipped downward. I used the foot pedals, and the boat turned left or right. This was awesome! It was like slipping behind the wheel of a Cadillac with power steering after driving an old, beat up car with no steering.

One unforeseen problem now presented itself. I had not been able to practice paddling with the new paddle and wasn't sure how efficient it would be. I had visualized myself slicing rapidly through the water with this new oar, the epitome of sleek, powerful movement. Unfortunately, the hybrid craft had higher sides than most traditional kayaks, and smooth, easy strokes did not seem possible. The oar bumped against the top of the sides with every curve, and I needed to radically change my stroke to a much higher arc. This higher arc also meant water dripping off the paddle into the kayak.

It soon became apparent that the one-sided graphite racing paddle worked better. Fortunately, because I was now controlling direction with the rudder, I could paddle from one side of the boat for more extended periods of time.

Nevertheless, I did manage a modicum of *glide* as I slowly crossed Lake Irving. Folks were out on houseboats, fishing and enjoying a pleasant Minnesota sunset. I was certain that no one relaxing on those boats had worked harder than I had this day.

I found the channel markings and slid beneath the bridge and out the other side. A huge lake appeared ahead of me. This was Lake Bemidji. Unsure which direction to paddle, I spotted an area off to my left with a few picnic tables and a playground.

My craft washed to shore, and I pulled out of the water and collapsed to the ground in great relief. I was not yet aware of it, but I had landed directly behind a large figure of Paul Bunyan and his partner in logging, Babe, the Blue Ox. I knew a section of river where their expertise was desperately needed. Lying on the ground, I wondered how it would ever be possible to describe to anyone what I had just been through for the past four days and nights.

Four ladies were sitting at a picnic table, watching their children playing nearby. They all had plates of food in front of them. I wanted nothing more than to find some food for myself. Gathering my exhausted body off the ground, I went in search of information.

"Where could I find lodging in this town?" I inquired of the ladies.

"You look like you could use some food," one said. Apparently, they were very intuitive, as most ladies are. Or perhaps it was just obvious.

I sighed. "Yes, food and a place to sleep. You have no idea what I've just come through."

I was humbled when one lady offered me food. They had Chinese takeout spread out on a table and she took a plate and passed it to me. I thanked them profusely and grabbed it without hesitation.

"Your best lodging will be found over there." They pointed to a site across the corner of Lake Bemidji.

The wind had picked up and a smattering of waves tried to press me back toward shore as I shoved off again. It was a one-mile crossing to Nymore Beach, where several lodging spots awaited.

I admit to some heart-pounding, adrenalin-powered paddling as I crossed over the corner of the lake. This time, the waves were a bit taller, but I kept close enough to the right shoreline that I believed I could swim safely to shore—should it become necessary.

Every stroke brought me closer to that blissful hotel room, a shower, and food. Unless you've been out in nature roughing it for an extended period of time, you cannot imagine what bliss is brought to weary souls by a hot shower and a comfortable bed.

I hit Nymore Beach exhausted, yet in high spirits. I had paddled 24 difficult miles that day and I was still alive.

Once in my room, I grabbed the plastic baggie with the dehydrated meals and pulled out my camera and phone. I was shocked and amazed when the camera screen came to life and, wonder of all wonders, the rice had worked and also extracted the moisture from the phone, which I used immediately to make a call. The folks back home seemed happy to once again hear from the creature that had arisen from the lagoon.

Chapter 10

My travels have taught me many things. Each adventure has been unique in its own way, but no matter the mode of travel or the destination, one basic tenet is always reinforced: *It's best to travel light.*

On the Appalachian Trail, I carried on my back everything needed for survival. I often felt like a beast of burden, a slave to that pack bulging from my body. I constantly attempted to find the delicate balance of survival and comfort. Of course I needed the essentials for survival, but I also wanted a few items of comfort, possessions that would make life more bearable—all while keeping the weight that burdened me to a minimum. My rule on the trail was that if I did not use an item every day, I sent it home.

On my bike ride across America, I faced similar choices. On that trip, the weight was packed into panniers attached to the bicycle frame. With the knowledge that my legs and not my shoulders would bear the brunt of the burden, I first filled those panniers to the breaking point. On the Appalachian Trail, my backpack weighed in on the first day at 35 pounds but was soon whittled down to 28 pounds. The weight in my bike panniers started at 40 pounds. As I lumbered over mountains and slogged through valleys on the Appalachian Trail, the weight I carried was atop me, pressing me downward. As I pedaled across the country, the 40 pounds in my bike panniers were all carried over my rear bike wheel— but it was weight dragging along behind me. I soon realized I did not enjoy pedaling uphill with excess baggage.

So as I rode from sea to shining sea, I determined to heed the advice of Hebrews 12:1 and rid myself of everything that hindered and the sin that so easily entangled me—the sin of excess weight. Four times as I crossed the fruited plain and mountains majestic, I wheeled up to a post office and released more and more stuff, stuff that was holding me back and making it more difficult to reach my goal of Key West, Florida. By the time I did my final weight cleansing in Monticello, Florida, I was carrying a bare-bones 15 pounds of weight.

Over mountains, through wilderness, baking in the hot desert sun, and drenched with downpours—all of this I'd endured, and apparently, I still had not absorbed the immutability of the creed, *Travel light.* When I planned my kayak trip, I reasoned that weight should not be a problem. The kayak has plenty of cargo space fore and aft. Furthermore, I was going to be on a flowing river where the current might very likely float me and my cargo merrily down the stream without much effort on my part. I filled my two waterproof bags to their fullest capacity with many extras.

I had not counted on the miseries of this swamp. And even though, once on shore, I did indeed have all my needs met by everything I'd stuffed into those bags, the weight had to be carried from kayak to campsite every evening and back again to the kayak in the morning. As you've already witnessed, just the thought of dragging everything through the woods discouraged me from portaging when such a course would have been wise.

So once again, I realized it was time to purge myself of all encumbrances.

In my luxurious hotel room following a luxurious shower I devoured a deliciously luxurious large pizza.

Then both bags were emptied and all contents were permitted a short time to present their arguments for being given a continued berth on my ship. The fishing rod and tackle didn't make the cut. I'm not a fisherman anyway. How had I even considered that I would use those? I had probably succumbed to a few visions of Tom Sawyer floating downstream with a fishing pole extended while napping in the sunshine.

When the sheep and goats had been separated, 20 pounds of excess baggage had been set aside to send home. My plan was to take a day off here in Bemidji, celebrating my survival of the swamp and resting up for the challenges to come. I knew there were some rather large lakes to be crossed in the near future, and I was keenly aware those lakes also came with dire warnings.

Luxuriating beneath freshly washed sheets, I grabbed my iPad. What were my sisters, brothers-in-law, and cousins experiencing on their bus trip? What was I missing? Several of my sisters had Facebook accounts, and they were documenting the trip. While I had traveled 60 miles in the swamp, that rollicking busload had been all over the West. Photos of Yellowstone National Park taunted me: *Look what you missed*.

They had traveled all the way to Banff, Canada, and witnessed many beautiful sights. I could just imagine all the laughter and stories they had shared on that bus. I also imagined the singing that broke forth every day. My family is blessed with much singing ability. How I missed my family. And to think I could have been a part of that! They had now reached the zenith of their trip and were on the journey back toward Ohio. I wondered where they had crossed the Mississippi River on their way west and where they might cross it on the road home.

While one strong motivation for my trips into the wilderness is having time alone for reflection, prayer, and growth, the solitude also becomes one of the greatest difficulties. The isolation always reminds me how important family and friends are to my existence. The most challenging part of every adventure has been dealing with acute loneliness.

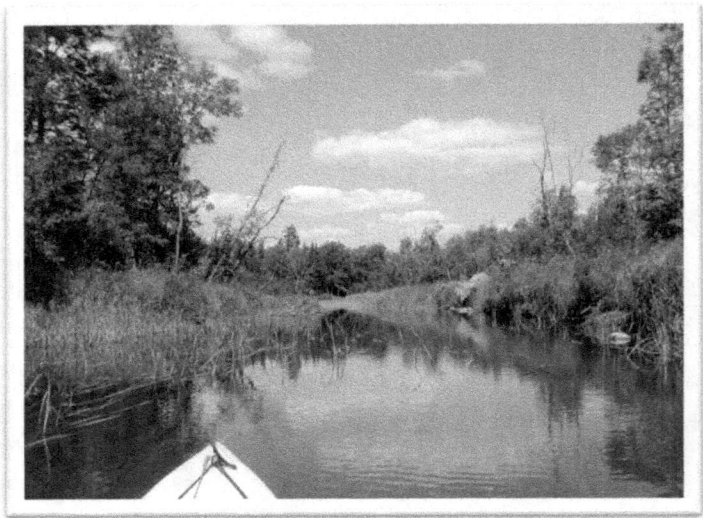

Chapter 11

In Hebrews, the apostle Paul reminds us that as we run our race of life, we should keep our eyes on our goal—Jesus—and strip off all extra weight that keeps us from running well. As we run, we are not isolated and alone. We are being cheered on by a "great cloud" of folks shouting encouragement to us. It's quite a different picture than my lonely travels.

But who is this crowd cheering from the clouds, and why are they interested in our race? To understand and marvel at this scene, we need only go back one chapter to Hebrews 11.

We know this as the faith chapter, where Paul speaks about some great men and women of faith.

The chapter begins with an explanation of what faith is: *being certain of what we don't see.* All of us who have had a loved one go ahead of us can be certain our loved one is there, cheering us on.

Paul starts by commending Abel, Enoch, and Noah for their faith. He spends a number of verses on the incredible faith of Abraham. That seems warranted, since Abe is named as the father of our faith. Then comes Isaac, Jacob, Joseph, and Moses. We are all familiar with the stories about these Old Testament heroes. Oh, what's this? Rahab the prostitute made the list of greats. That bodes well for us struggling folks, trying to understand and live faith. What great thing did this lady of the evening do? She simply was obedient and hid some spies. Perhaps it's not as difficult to be a Christ follower as some folks would make it.

There is something missing, however, from each of these stories, even Abraham's. The chapter presents a picture of *incompleteness.* Once we understand that, we also understand the crowd's apparent interest in our race and why they encourage us to travel as light as possible.

These folks all lived their lives of faith before Jesus arrived on the scene. When God's promise of a Savior was fulfilled on a night in Bethlehem and a cross in Jerusalem, every one of these folks mentioned had already departed the earth. They had received and held onto a promise about a coming Messiah who would heal the world and perfect their relationship with God, but they passed on before that promise was fulfilled.

We, however, are living after the coming of the Savior of mankind. Today we have the promise of being made perfect through Jesus.

That sounds impossible. It sounds too good to be true. And highly unlikely. Believe me, I had tried to find the route to perfection, and all the roads I took just led to frustration.

Do you remember the opening of the story of Job? A group of angels presented themselves to God, and for some reason Satan showed up with them. I'm not sure why he was even there, but I suspect that wherever the angels were doing good, Satan was attempting to disrupt things.

God asked the evil one where he had been.

"Oh, I've just been roaming through the earth, going back and forth in the world."

"Have you noticed my servant Job down there on earth? He is one of a kind, blameless and upright."

I can imagine Satan scoffing.

"Yes, but that's because you have put a hedge of protection around him. Just look at the good life you've given him."

In the book of Job, we can read about what happened: That conversation led to a challenge presented and accepted.

But as this author trudges over mountains and through valleys on his own quest to understand the meaning of following Christ, a similar scene has often inspired and helped him.

In the scenario I imagine, Satan again presents himself to God, this time chortling about the missteps and mishaps of said author.

God agrees to humor old Beelzebub and takes a glance in my direction.

"I can't see him," says God. "But I know He belongs to my Son."

He calls for Jesus.

"Would you stand here in front of me?" He requests of His Son.

As Jesus steps in, God looks through Him and sees me clearly.

"Perfection!" He shouts. "This guy's perfect!"

Satan slinks away in defeat once again.

Now, the thought that I, your humble writer of words, am perfect is a thought that stretches all credulity. It not only stretches but probably breaks credulity into a thousand pieces.

Jesus came to earth to do one thing—to do away with the poison Satan spread throughout God's good creation and put between God and humanity. Jesus sacrificed Himself on the cross to make us perfect in God's sight, even though we still need a lot of scrubbing and cleaning up.* All of those heroes of faith mentioned in the first part of Hebrews 11 looked forward to the promise of a Savior who would mend perfectly their relationship to the Creator. They ran their races with persistence and determination because they believed God would keep His promise. But it is *our* race now that completes and finishes God's plan to make our relationship with Him perfect, just as He promised. Without our stories and our lives of faith, the full promises of God are not yet complete.

Both the Old Testament witnesses of faith and all of us who are living perfect lives in Christ are needed to complete God's work of redeeming and renewing His creation. The last verse in Chapter 11 of Hebrews says that only together with *us* would this great cloud of the faithful be made perfect. *Our stories* finish the great Faith Chapter! The perfection we've been given moves the story forward toward the final ending God has planned.

That's a big wow there! Those in the huge cheering throng—and I believe our loved ones are among them—are waiting for us to ditch everything holding us back so that we can run like the wind toward the finish line. They're urging us on because we are the ingredient still necessary for the completion of God's promises.

----

* Hebrews 10:14. "For by one sacrifice he has made perfect forever those who are being made holy."

This is how I'm running my race. Still learning what to shed so that I can travel light. Still imperfect. But knowing that God isn't looking at my imperfection. He's looking at Christ's perfection.

Chapter 12

The next day in Bemidji, Minnesota, I had nothing to do but visit the post office, stroll about town, eat, and think about what lay ahead.

The Mississippi River channel leaving Lake Bemidji lay three miles across the lake from Nymore Beach. My map had the warning printed in red: *Paddling across the lake is not recommended; if you must do so, stay close to shore.*

"I must do so," I said to the map.

Back in my kayak the next morning, I noticed that it rode just a bit higher. The 20 pounds I'd dropped off at the post office had cut my load by a third. Tentatively, I rowed my craft out into deeper water, always with an eye on the shore. For an hour I paddled within swimming distance of solid ground. According to the map, the point at which the river exited the lake should have been within sight. It certainly showed up clearly on paper. But out on the lake, surrounded by bulrushes and other lake weeds, the channel was invisible. I needed to paddle farther out into the lake to get a better visual of what lay ahead.

Or had I somehow missed it?

A quagmire of water lilies, bulrushes, and various unknown pointy foliage protruding from the lake lay between me and clear visibility. I slowly plowed my way through this new maze. A sudden explosion of water and wings startled me as I surprised an assembly of ducks. My heart raced wildly for a few moments, and then I proceeded more cautiously.

Once free from the foliage and now a good distance out into the lake, I spied what looked like the channel exit, and I at last did reach the small area where the Mississippi left the lake and flowed freely. For a mile, the river ran sufficiently deep so that it was almost a pleasurable paddle. Was this trip perhaps about to get easier?

In the distance, I saw an elderly man wading in the middle of the river. A small plastic kayak floated nearby. I drifted toward him, eager to at last meet another river kayaker.

Jerry was not a recreational kayaker. He explained that he was out catching redtail chubs. These are small bait fish, approximately four inches long, that he sold to bait shops for $14 a dozen. He had the licensed rights to this section of the river, and it had been his part-time occupation for the past 60 years.

Jerry had come from the opposite direction, and I inquired about the river conditions I was about to encounter. I explained about the shallow water I had overcome so far.

"It's not going to get better for a number of miles," he said. "I can float in six inches of water with my small boat, and it grounded out several times this morning. Once you get closer to Stump Lake you should be all right."

Stump Lake is held back by a dam constructed in 1909 to provide electricity for the city of Bemidji. It's merely a formality today, providing less than one percent of Bemidji's electrical power. I knew that this would also be the first time I had no choice but to portage. I doubted that the same strategy I had used at the log dams and the beaver dams would be advisable at this dam.

For the next few miles, I enjoyed a walk in the river. With rope in hand, I strolled the Mississippi while my watercraft floated at times in front of me and at times beside me. Every now and then it needed an encouraging tug to grind across rocks. Ankle deep in water, I splashed a few more miles toward the Mississippi delta, still several thousand miles away.

As I neared Stump Lake, the water deepened and the kayak finally floated freely. In this stretch, I now also reached the northernmost point of the Mississippi River and finally started bending toward the south. My joy in all of this was tempered, though, by the knowledge that just ahead of me was the dam that would force my first portage. This time, I would have no alternative.

I was surprised to find that the dam holding back Stump Lake did not have a strenuous job. My fears had swirled around visions of vicious currents sucking me into turbines, but those worries dissipated as I neared the structure. The lake itself was nothing more than a widening of the river; here, it was almost five times the width it had been, and the water was placid. The scene was actually quite picturesque, and I detected no threat from the current. Across the top of the dam, where I assumed the water dropped away to a lower level, a walkway lined with railings crossed the river. Off to one side, a square block building stood guard over the scene.

To my right, I saw the sign depicting a person carrying a canoe, with the word PORTAGE in large letters above the sketch. This was the designated take-out place. I pulled up on the grassy bank and assembled the cart that would transport the kayak.

The portage around Stump Lake went smoothly. I pulled the cart and kayak up a short slope and discovered the pathway that then led down a steep hill and back to the river below the dam. Before long, I was again floating down the Mississippi.

The dreaded challenges of dams and portages had risen up and taken shape in reality—but I had faced the situation and had done what needed to be done, and the experience had not turned out as badly as I had imagined. With my relief came more confidence. I told myself that I could handle whatever situation the river presented to me.

This happens so often in life. When we finally face our fears and deal with them, we find there was not as much danger or disaster as we had cooked up with all of our worrying.

I drifted along for a few miles, exulting in my victory and enjoying the pleasant surroundings and easy navigation in these waters. Still, my worries were not entirely gone. I knew there was a series of dams coming up that would require piloting my craft through locks—a total of 27 dams. Of even more concern were the three lakes that I would cross this day, all much larger than Stump Lake. I was hoping to end the day on an island in the middle of the third lake.

There are two places in the world where an island in a lake includes another lake on the island. Star Island is one of those two places. This island, located close to the middle of Cass Lake, has a body of water of considerable size within its interior—Lake Windigo. That lake on an island within a lake roused my curiosity. I would never get another chance to see this singular marvel, and so I planned to camp on Star Island that night.

Cass Lake is seven miles wide; a three-mile paddle into the lake would land me on Star Island's southern shore, where my map showed a campsite for watercraft. I would take time to check out the lake on Star Island, and the next day, I could finish the four-mile stretch to the northeastern corner of Cass Lake where the Mississippi leaves this chain of lakes and continues south.

As I rounded a bend, Wolf Lake opened up before me. I scanned its shores, attempting to locate the channel where the Mississippi exited this lake. No outlet presented itself. Far off in the distance, a little spit of land jutted out into the water. It was over a mile away, and I tentatively paddled out further in the lake. Some gentle swells greeted me, but there was nothing too frightening. As I approached that spit of land, I saw that it was merely a sandbar. Perhaps the river's outlet was just around the sandbar. Unfortunately, the wind picked up and made paddling almost impossible. I bent into the wind and the waves, but could not round that sandbar.

Giving up, I allowed the wind to ground me on the white beach. A houseboat had tied up there as well. As I pulled my kayak up on the sand, a man on the boat shouted a greeting. His wife and two daughters and several grandkids were nearby, playing on the beach. He invited me to come onboard, offered a drink, and encouraged me to make a sandwich from provisions in the ice chest. I gladly accepted the hospitality.

"I'm looking for the spot where the Mississippi flows out of this lake," I said between bites of sandwich.

He laughed and said, "You've come a mile too far." Pointing back in the direction I had just come, he directed my attention

70

to a small indentation in the shore, not very far from where I had entered Wolf Lake.

At least I had the wind at my back as I backtracked. I'd done two extra miles, but I was back on the river. I lamented the misfortune of those extra miles, but my conversation on the houseboat had given me useful information about the next two lakes, and for that I was grateful.

The second lake for the day was Lake Andrusia. The houseboat captain had told me exactly where to find the river channel. "When you enter Lake Andrusia, look over to your right. About a mile distant, you'll see a bridge. Head directly to that bridge, and you'll be back on the river for a short distance before reaching Allen's Bay," he had told me.

Allen's Bay was the beginning of the third lake, Cass Lake. The captain had words of caution about that body of water.

"Cass Lake can be dangerous," he had warned. "Where are you planning to spend the night?"

"I hope to end up on Star Island."

I could see him cringe. He warned me to be very careful. "When the wind picks up, you don't want to be out on that lake."

On the map, Lake Andrusia is configured much like the duodenum of your small intestine. I entered the digestive tract along the southwestern shore and saw the bridge the captain had mentioned. I set a course toward the southeastern corner of the duodenum. Still, this took me a good distance from shore. The lake was a bit choppy, and my senses were on high alert. *Just keep paddling, look straight ahead, don't panic. Your boat's made for these conditions.* All these and other thoughts cycled through my mind as I paddled through what looked like one-foot rollers. The boat and I did well, and Lake Andrusia digested me and passed me on through to Cass Lake.

But if Andrusia is the beginning of the small intestine, Cass Lake is the entire length of the digestive system, and that day, it was waiting to break me down and consume me.

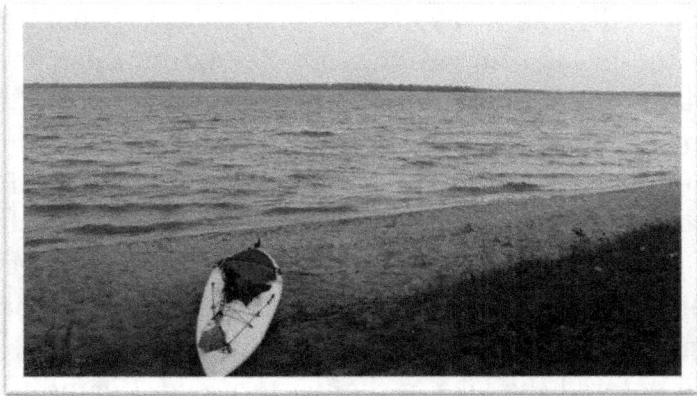

Chapter 13

Entering Allen's Bay at the western end of Cass Lake, I paused to consult my map. I wanted to be certain of my directions before committing my kayak to the deep. In this monster of a lake, I could see two bodies of land far off to my left. Those were the Potato Islands. Even farther off in the distance was a larger land mass that I hoped was Star Island.

On the big blue blob representing Cass Lake, my map gave its warning in red letters: *Paddlers are advised to respect the power of the wind on a large lake and stay away from the center. If you must paddle, stick to the shoreline. The lake can be dangerous and winds rise unexpectedly.*

I had just read truth and was about to live that truth. The Bible advises that if you sow to the wind, you'll reap the whirlwind. I sowed and reaped that day. The winds did rise unexpectedly and I was headed for the center—not only the center of the lake but also the center of extreme danger.

Paddling along Allen's Bay, I kept the shoreline within reasonable distance. The water was choppy, but I had already conquered two other lakes this day and I was certain that the island far out there in the distance was my goal, Star Island.

Many automobile mirrors bear a warning: "Objects are closer than they appear." On a lake, it's just the opposite: "Islands are farther away than they appear." Much farther.

I'd entered the lake at the western end. I determined to stay close to the northern shore as long as possible before committing to paddling the open stretch of water across to the island. Feeling fairly confident, I rounded a small spit of ground and saw a dock and a few campers on the shore.

Perhaps I should abandon the push for the island and find a camping spot here, suggested the sensible part of my brain.

But you have to get across this lake somehow, the stubborn part of me argued, *and you want to see that island with a lake on it. You'll never have another chance, if you don't do it now.*

To get to the camping site on the island, though, I would have to turn south and actually swing around the tip of Star Island. The commitment was made, and I moved away from the northern shore of the lake and headed for the southern end of the island and a hoped-for campsite. That might have been the worst decision I have ever made.

As I paddled south, farther out into the lake and away from the protecting shore, I felt the wind picking up force, blowing directly in my face. What had been one-foot swells rapidly grew larger. Soon I was too far from shore to swim to safety in the event of disaster. Then, as though the elements and the lake had been waiting for me to venture out, the wind picked up even more and the waves rose up to terrifying heights.

Every fourth or fifth wave arrived with a snarling curl of white and slammed against the kayak. Gripping my paddle with a death grip, I plunged it into the water again and again, trying to counteract the fury of the wind and waves. I attempted to point my boat toward the island but had to keep a careful eye on the angle of the approaching waves. I did not want to get swamped, but, frankly, had very little idea how to avoid it. Using the rudder, I stomped the foot pedal furiously, left or right, trying to keep the kayak headed into the waves and giving the lake no chance to broadside my craft.

Pray and paddle, pray and paddle. Watch that third wave coming at you. Adrenalin rushed through every inch of my body and my senses were heightened as never before in my life. On my Appalachian Trail hike, I had clung to a maple tree as a tornado raged around me. That day, I thought I might die. But that experience paled to the fear that now rode with me. There was a very real possibility that I would die here on this lake and never see my family again. I could have been on a bus with my family and cousins, joking and laughing and singing, but instead I was out here fighting for my life. I prayed with desperation. I pleaded with God. I bargained with God.

"Get me off this lake alive, and I'll do whatever You ask of me."

Of course, I was thinking of my friend Ivan's dream. Had he been given a premonition of my death? His prayer for my safety had been so intense, and he had been very somber when he told me, "You don't have to do this." Had he known? Was this how my life was going to end?

I thought, too, of the request that had been made of me just before I left. A man was dying of cancer, his days were numbered, and his family wanted to preserve his story in written form. I had turned down the opportunity with little thought, never asking God whether this might be something He wanted me to do. Now, because I had been so determined to follow my own plan, my remaining time on this earth might only be numbered in minutes, not even days.

And I recalled, again and again, how the man that sold me the kayak had assured me it rode four-foot waves on Lake Michigan. Could I trust it to do that for me on Cass Lake?

Every time a huge wave washed over my bow, I exclaimed, "I'm still alive!" Fortunately, I had the front portion of the canvas spray skirt snapped into place, and most of the water flowed across my bow rather than filling up the cockpit. For two hours, the battle between man and nature raged. I was determined to survive. *I will see my family again. As long as I'm afloat, I've got a chance.* My knuckles were swollen and my hands were cramping from the desperate grip on the paddle. Blisters were already forming on my fingers.

I would soon have to make that dangerous maneuver, trying to paddle out past the southern tip of the island and then turning sharply to the left to head back toward the beach. That turn would expose the entire right side of my kayak to the buffeting waves. Would it be able to ride the waves, or would this be my shipwreck? The time was near to make that call.

"Do it now!" I screamed.

Slamming the foot pedal, I paddled furiously on the right side to turn the kayak toward the island.

A giant wave immediately broadsided the kayak. I knew this was the moment I was going to die.

But a beautiful thing happened. The Sea Clipper rose right up and over that wave. My stomach drained down to my ankles as the wave dropped me down into its trench. One more rise and drop, and my kayak was turned toward the island and headed directly toward the beach. I was surfing the waves as they hit me from behind.

The man in Chicago was right; this boat could ride the waves!

I realized I was going to live. My kayak rushed toward the beach and soon came to an abrupt stop. I was alive and on solid ground. I pulled my craft up on the shore and fell face down, inhaling a mouthful of sand as I lay there, trembling and relieved.

Exhausted, I pulled myself to a nearby picnic table and sat there, overwhelmed with awe of what I had come through and wonder that I was still alive. I sat for a long time, unable to go about my usual chores of erecting a tent and cooking a meal. I briefly thought of the lake on this island that I had been determined to see, and immediately dismissed it. I no longer cared.

Eventually, I did make camp, and I set up my tent and cooked a hot meal. But I never did see the silly lake on an island in a lake.

I was alive, and that was all that mattered.

In the far corners of my mind lurked the gloomy fact that I was on an island and had a four-mile paddle awaiting me the next day, but my conscious thoughts entertained the idea of homesteading right there and never again boarding any kind of ship, boat, canoe, kayak, raft, or inner tube.

Chapter 14

Sleep was elusive. If you've ever spent a day on the lake fishing, you will understand the feeling—all night, undulating waves rolled beneath me, and my tent seemed to rock as much as my boat had done. Exhausted, my mind played back, over and over, the vision of the menacing waves coming at me. When sleep finally came, I dreamed I was in a boat, frightened and paddling furiously.

Morning did arrive, though, and the lake seemed to have calmed down a bit. I looked out across the water at the opposite shore and the placid surface gave me hope that it would be an uneventful four-mile paddle.

Skirting the island and staying close to the beach, I passed several docks. Here were small, quaint summer cottages set back from the water. Artists and writers frequented these retreats on Star Island.

I continued to paddle north, trying to determine the best place to angle across Cass Lake toward the eastern shore where I would portage around Knutson Dam and put this monster lake behind me forever.

The opposite land mass was faintly visible in the distance. I prayed for a safe crossing and struck out toward that shore.

The waves were perhaps a foot or two, but after yesterday's terrifying crossing, this seemed moderate. My kayak had proved it could carry me across this stretch. If I just kept paddling and trusted my boat, I would arrive safely. The waves were hitting me from behind. I hoped they would push me more quickly toward my goal. Still, I felt a clutching fear.

An hour passed, and the opposite shore did not appear to be any closer. I cast a glance behind me, and there was Star Island, still quite large and visible.

Finally, several hours into my paddle, the opposite shore at last came into sharper focus and Star Island had receded to a thin line on the horizon behind me.

Then the wind picked up again. It did not have the force of the previous day, but the gusts still kicked up some powerful waves. I found myself constantly glancing behind me, assessing the oncoming waves like someone anticipating an ambush.

The waves were now at least three feet, rolling beneath me, with the larger ones lifting the kayak and turning it into a surf board. My mind turned briefly to the Bible's account of Jesus walking on the water in a storm, and I prayed again for safety and reminded God that I really did not have enough faith to duplicate Jesus' walk.

My fear and anxiety edged toward pure terror. But stroke by stroke, prayer by prayer, I paddled on.

You can imagine my relief at the sight of a fishing boat lumbering through the waves about a mile offshore. It was headed toward Star Island, and I paddled at an angle to intercept it. I shouted a good morning.

"I'm not a very experienced kayaker. Would you keep an eye on me?" They assured me they would, and I was greatly comforted in knowing there was someone nearby who had the means of rescue, should that be necessary.

Rounding a small, man-made rock barrier extending outward from the shore, I was suddenly in calm water.

"I'm alive!" I shouted. "I did it! Thank you, Jesus!"

I would live to paddle another day. Hallelujah, my troubles were over. Nothing but blue skies and calm waters from now on, I mused.

As I tugged my boat around Knutson Dam, I walked through the Knutson Dam Recreation Area. Many of the 40 camping sites were filled, and I found myself and my kayak an object of curiosity. This was the first audience with whom I could share my death-defying exploits on Cass Lake, and they were properly amazed, most of them aware how dangerous that lake can be.

Friendly campers pointed me in the right direction. They also warned that the river flowing away from the dam was quite low. That was fine with me. I would have been quite happy to find it bone dry.

There was more information to be gleaned at the campground. I learned that several miles ahead I'd find an area known as Mississippi Meadows. There, the river widens and is home to many ducks and other waterfowl. I would also have to navigate through rice fields as I neared Lake Winnibigoshish.

Rice fields? That seemed odd. Nothing in my research had suggested I would have to maneuver through rice paddies.

However, I did know plenty about Lake Winnibigoshish, known to locals as Lake Winnie. The map stamps it with the usual warnings about high wind, waves, and dangerous and hazardous conditions. "Paddling across this lake is not recommended," read the warning. I had no intention of paddling across Minnesota's fourth-largest lake. While the state is known as the land of 10,000 lakes, in reality the state has 11,842 lakes larger than 10 acres. Lake Winnie was 15 miles across. I would take as long as needed to skirt around the lake, but I would not attempt a direct crossing.

My plan was to enter the lake, hug the shore to the south, find a camping spot for that night, and then spend the following day circumnavigating the lake in a counterclockwise direction until I reached the Winnie Dam.

But that was tomorrow. Today, I embraced the low water in the river below Knutson Dam. I had no fear of waves washing over me. Occasionally a little riffle tickled my ankles when I got out to tug the kayak over rocks.

Eventually, as my camper informants had predicted, the river deepened and widened. The wind also picked up and a headwind attempted to push me back toward Cass Lake. I soldiered on, believing that this river could not surprise me anymore.

But surprise me it did when I came into view of thousands of acres of wild rice growing in the river.

For a short time, I was able to follow the channel of the river, but soon it disappeared and I was floating in a vast field of amber waves of grain with absolutely no navigational cues. I paddled in the direction I believed was correct, but the wind conspired with the rice fields and totally confused me. Forcing my way down one narrow channel through weeds and rice, I seemed to have hit a dead end, so I backed my kayak out and set off in a new direction in the labyrinth.

Once again, I implored a higher power for assistance.

"God, it's me again. You got me over the lake, now I'm lost—in a rice field, of all things. Guide me out of this latest mess."

I really can't say if there was an *Amen* or not, because it seemed the last two days had been a continual prayer of desperation, never actually ending one prayer before finding another urgently necessary.

The wind had blown me in a complete circle. I realized that when I caught sight of the same channel through the weeds that I had tried before. How could I be so confused, so totally disoriented? I know it sounds incredible—being lost in a rice field—but you can't know how confusing it is until you spend a day trying to find your way through a rice maze where every stalk looks exactly the same as the next and there are no street signs or highway markers.

Something in my soul—yes, I do believe it was a suggestion from God—prompted me. *Look to your right. That small opening that goes through the tall weeds choking that section of rice plants. Go through there.*

That small opening was the same channel I had tried earlier and then backed out of when I decided it went nowhere.

I bent against the paddle, forcing my vessel into the headwind until, for the second time, I entered the small opening in the weeds. It was about the width of my kayak. I took another look and decided to push through. Even if it was a tunnel to nowhere, it was protected from the wind that seemed determined to blow me about.

Emerging at the other end of the tunnel, I was thrilled at the sight of a distant building perched on a bank. I set out in the direction of that building and soon rediscovered the main river channel. Gradually the rice thinned out and a proper river once again emerged.

What's next? I wondered. *The Enchanted Forest?*

The hours passed. Morning became afternoon, and there was nowhere to stop even for a snack. Wind and waves still lashed my boat, but two-foot river waves no longer concerned me. I had been through so much worse. In addition, the riverbank was clearly visible and its nearness gave me a tangible sense of safety.

Evening was coming on, and I suspected—I hoped—that I was nearing Lake Winnie. Along the river I spotted the cottages of a fishing camp—they're called *resorts* in the lakes region. I greeted several men on one of the docks and asked if I was close to Lake Winnie.

"Straight ahead, about a half mile," they said.

All I needed now was enough stamina to enter the lake, paddle to my right, and find a camping spot.

But the wind was determined to have the last word that day. As I entered the opening to the lake, I was hit with gusts of such force that I found it impossible to paddle to the right. After a few brief moments of fighting, I surrendered. I was hungry and exhausted. At that moment, I did not care where the elements took me. Pulling in my paddle, I let the wind and waves propel the kayak and I used the rudder to steer toward the shoreline—the shore in the *opposite* direction I had intended to take. Staying about 200 feet from land, I searched for a place to pull out, but a three-foot concrete barrier erected at the edge of the water to inhibit erosion made beaching my craft impossible.

Wait a minute, what's that above the wall?

I took a second look—and it was not a mirage. There was a campground with campers parked among the sites. I had no way of reaching this oasis, though. The waves crashed against the barrier. I briefly thought of sacrificing the kayak—let it smash to pieces against that wall, and I'll jump out at just the precise moment and scamper up and over it to safety. The idea actually made some sense at the time. I was physically and mentally at the breaking point.

The barrier ended just shy of a short dock jutting out into the waves. Behind the dock, a small road led away from the water and I could see the last site in the campground—and it was vacant. My life suddenly took a turn for the better. I was home for the night.

As I dragged my kayak from knee-deep water, I suffered one final assault from the lake. Blood streamed down my left leg from a gash a few inches below my knee. Apparently, some sea creature had helped himself to a bite of supper.

Pulling the kayak into the campsite, I realized why this spot was unclaimed. The campground outhouses were within smelling distance. I cared not a whit. Here I would even have a picnic table. In spite of the odors drifting about, this was luxury.

I hoped the cut on my leg would cease bleeding before draining my body of all plasma. However, the river of red showed no signs of slowing. Taking out my small first aid kit, I applied several band-aids, but the blood soon seeped through and trickled down over my sandal.

Without a Plan B for medical treatment, I set about erecting my tent and tried to ignore the fact that I was probably bleeding to death. At one point I paused for just a moment to check the blood-soaked band-aids—and looked up to see the wind tumbling my tent across the grassy area of the campsite.

It just never stops.

Forget the tent. Could I sleep in the kayak? Back home in Ohio, I had tried stretching out in the cockpit, testing the space. Sleeping there would be possible, but not comfortable.

My stubbornness won out. I retrieved the tent. Finding a suitable tree, I lashed the tent to it and secured the ground stakes.

As I finished and stood back to review my work, around the bend in the road came an apparition, headed straight for my camp. Was I really seeing this or was my fatigue playing tricks on me? I took a closer look. Not a hallucination, but— yes, it really was a young Conservative Mennonite couple. In the tradition of my own upbringing, the lady wore a long, modest dress and a head covering.

How could I have landed in the middle of a Mennonite encampment? I immediately called out to them and learned that several families from their church were there at the campground.

"Why don't you join us for supper? We have a fire going and have plenty of hot dogs and hamburgers."

No prodding was necessary. I immediately accepted the invitation.

The young man noticed the blood still flowing freely down my leg.

"You've got yourself a nasty cut."

I explained that I thought something had taken a bite out of me while I pulled the kayak out of the water. "This lake's infested with zebra mussels," he replied. "They're razor sharp. You might have stumbled into some of those."

His words reminded me that an elderly couple back at Cass Lake had warned me about an infestation at Lake Winnie. I knew nothing about zebra mussels, but I did know my lifeblood was still oozing out of me and the wound was beginning to itch unbearably.

Nothing could deter me, though, from partaking of good food and comforting camaraderie. Less than an hour later, I was part of a campfire circle made up of three generations of Mennonites. The fellowship with these folks made me even more aware of how alone I was and how much I missed my family.

The pastor of the Mennonite church was among the group. He asked how I planned to get across Lake Winnie.

"You do know that it's not safe to paddle across?"

I assured him that such a plan was not even under consideration, adding, "The way this wind is blowing, it's barely safe to paddle close to shore."

I thought for a brief moment and then did the unthinkable.

"Would any of you have a truck and trailer that I could hire to transport me around the lake?"

On each of my previous quests, voicing that question would have been a commission of sacrilege. My father always taught me to do a task right, taking no shortcuts. On my hike of the Appalachian Trail, I made that demand of myself, hiking as a purist. That meant I passed every white blaze marking the official trail from Georgia to Maine. Yes, there were easier trails, shortcuts, and detours—they were marked with blue blazes. Other hikers sometimes hitchhiked—that was called yellow blazing. I followed the white blazes religiously. Two years later, on my bicycle ride across America, I pedaled every mile of the way, accepting no rides. I did come close one day in Colorado, when I encountered road construction and I thought I might be required to load my bike onto the back of a pickup to ride through that stretch. I was quite relieved and grateful when the workers stopped all traffic and allowed me weave my bike through the maze of paving equipment.

Now I heard myself inquire about a hitch around this lake. The purist in me raised an alarm; the exhausted part of me assured the purist that if I ever actually did arrive in New Orleans, I would drive back up to Lake Winnie and officially complete my journey of every mile of the Mississippi River. The purist backed down with no argument.

That night, lying in a tent no longer rolling on wild seas or tumbling about the beach in the wind, I marveled at how God had worked things out for me. I had fought to paddle to the right but instead had been blown left, right into a camp full of hospitable Christian folks.

Chapter 15

Pastor Bob arrived early the next morning as I took down my camp. The sight of the truck and trailer, waiting to transport my kayak, hit me with the reality of my choice. I gazed out over a placid Lake Winnie and lamented my decision the night before. *I could paddle this.*

I voiced that thought to Pastor Bob.

He gave me a look that I'm sure he reserves for comments bordering on insanity.

"Do you really think that would be smart?"

He did not give me a chance to debate.

"I'm here with the trailer, and we're going to portage you around this lake."

Thus, instead of a 20-mile paddle around the edge of the lake, I took the 60-mile portage on land. I did briefly consider justifying this as a required portage, but that did not quite satisfy my purist's desire to paddle every inch of this stinking, surprise-a-minute river.

The drive also meant that we had time to play the Mennonite game.

Movie buffs play a game known as "six degrees of Kevin Bacon." The premise is that any two people on earth can be connected by linking six or fewer acquaintances. The Kevin Bacon game links Hollywood personalities. The Mennonites have their own version—and I'm quite certain they were entertaining themselves in this way long before Hollywood ever thought of it.

Many Mennonites across America can trace their roots to the same pilgrims who first came to this country. But the Mennonite game is played even by those who are completely unaware of the generations who came before them. So many of us share similar last names that we know chances are good that we can find a connection somewhere—usually in only two or three degrees. Someone has heard of your grandfather or perhaps is married to the sister of the neighbor of your best friend.

Pastor Bob started the game.

"You're a Stutzman. I worked in Pennsylvania a number of years ago with a fellow by that name."

Sure enough, he knew and had worked with my first cousin.

One degree, and we're done. We Mennonites are much more practiced at this game than Hollywood.

Pastor Bob's portage service ended several hundred feet beyond the outlets of Winnie Dam, where a concrete ramp launched me and my kayak back into the waters of the Mississippi.

The river was quite shallow here. In spite of its size, Lake Winnie certainly seemed reluctant to give up much of its water. For a short time I bumped along the river bottom until at last I came into deeper water.

The shallowness of the river also matched a shallowness I was beginning to feel concerning this quest of conquering the mighty Mississippi. Something had changed. Perhaps the relentless challenges I had faced were beginning to wear down my resolve. The purist in me had caved in the night before with very little pressure. Being willing to skip a section of the journey was not part of my character. How could I have allowed myself to do that? On my previous journeys, my determination and stubbornness had always kept me going, but now I felt only a great mental weariness.

Something had happened that I couldn't quite understand.

As the river widened and deepened, so did my emotions. It was the aloneness that was getting to me. I had sat around that campfire with moms and dads while children ran about, and my own children and grandchildren were a thousand miles away. Their ordinary days of growing up were slipping by while I hiked and biked and fought rivers. What was I missing? I'm fortunate enough to still have my own mom and dad; they live less than five miles from my house, and I and my sisters can still go "home" to the house where we all grew up. But my parents are aging. Their days are slipping by, too. I even had a busload of relatives who had invited me to three weeks of fun with them. Yes, I was beginning to wish I had chosen the bus trip instead of life in this kayak.

They were on their way home. Where, I wondered, would they be crossing the Mississippi on the return trip? The likely crossing would be in Memphis, Tennessee. I had driven across the river there myself, numerous times in my travels. But Memphis was still weeks away for me and my kayak.

For the first time I was living the Mississippi River paddle dream I had envisioned. Otters poked their heads from the water and splashed about, warning others about the intruder. On a bank to my right, a flock of geese rested, and I glided toward them, wondering how close I could get. But they saw me at once, and with an explosion of honks and flapping wings, they scattered ahead of my kayak.

93

It was beautiful and so peaceful—yet my spirit was flagging. It didn't help that I was being offered up as a sacrifice to the local insects. I accepted the fact that I was the intruder in their environment. This was their home, and I was just a buffet passing through. I managed to kill a few, but for every warrior that died, 10 others had a meal.

Off to my right, a splendid sight presented itself. I wondered how many other nature sightings had gone unnoticed while I was preoccupied with the perils of progress, but this one I did not miss. Perched high in a tree top, an alopecia eagle surveyed its domain. The sight of the majestic bird brought back a stream of memories of mundane happenings. I could almost hear Mary murmur, "Alopecia."

Alopecia eagle, you say? You think you have never heard of it?

Well, yes, you have—you've just never heard the bird identified with this term.

At the time Mary and I were married, she was employed in the medical records department of the local hospital. Her job was to transcribe charts written by the doctors and convert them to a legible, typed form. Sometimes, she felt as though she was trying to interpret hieroglyphics on cave walls, but with time she became quite adept at discerning the meaning of each doctor's scribbles. When she was stumped by a term, she would peruse a medical journal, seeking the meaning of the word.

One day, a doctor remarked that she might not understand his description of a patient who had alopecia.

Mary immediately replied, "Oh, the guy's bald."

94

The doctor was impressed at her knowledge, and my wife was feeling quite proud of herself. That evening, she regaled me with the story.

Ho hum, I thought. *What's the big deal?*

It actually was a big deal for this reason: I had to listen to that word throughout our 32 years of marriage. Every time Mary spotted a man or an occasional lady that was balding, I heard her remark, "Alopecia."

The bald eagle brought back all those memories, and as I recalled how Mary delighted in telling me the story, I was soon pondering the importance of communication in marriage.

Couples often forget why they fell in love in the first place. They laugh and play and *talk* during courtship—Mary and I certainly did a lot of that—and then they get married and forget to laugh and play and talk—we did that, too. It's easy to drift away from those things when the stresses of kids, debts, jobs, and other distractions come our way.

But one of the complications of communication in marriage is that we men and women have two very different purposes for talking.

Ladies want to be heard; they want to be listened to. It seems that the most important thing for them in conversation is that someone is listening to them. They want to know that their feelings, needs, and problems are understood.

We men, on the other hand, see conversation as a method of solving problems and fixing things. Thus, halfway through a conversation, a man's mind is already churning with ideas on how to fix what we assume needs to be fixed. Our brains are so busy coming up with a solution that we miss the point: she just wants to get everything off her mind by talking about it. Wife talks to Hubby so that he knows what she is thinking and how she feels. But off we husbands go with solution in hand— and we often mess things up even worse than before.

The problem lies in that word *assume*. Men, our assumption is wrong. Women do not expect us to have an answer and solution for everything they want to talk about. As a matter of fact, they don't even *want* us to constantly offer our wise advice and share our vast knowledge. If we men could just learn to shut up and not try to fix everything, we could have an easier marriage. And there's a bonus—we won't actually be required to solve every problem!

Allow me to offer a different approach.

When your beloved is trying to explain something to you that you have absolutely no chance whatsoever to fix, I recommend doing this: Put one hand on your chin and tilt your head to one side and softly go, "Hmm." Allow her to continue explaining the unfixable, and slightly nod your head. This can be done with hand still on chin or removed. Do not look around or act uninterested—even if you are. (And chances are, you may be uninterested.) Do look directly into her eyes and say, "I understand." (You probably don't, or can't, understand, but that's complicating the issue.) A question here or there may not hurt, but keep those to a minimum. Too many questions, and you'll get far too much information.

There's one more get-out-of-jail-free card you can use if you get stuck in the weeds too deeply. Ask this question: "How do you see this situation turning out—if you could have a perfect scenario?" Chances are, you'll get the precise answer that's needed without further ado.

Above all, don't forget your mission. This is not about fixing anything. It's about listening to the lady in your life.

Ladies, we men aren't that hard to figure out, either. All we require is a modicum of respect and affirmation. Here's a secret: One simple compliment will give us enough fuel to take us through an entire day.

I still remember an afternoon when I arrived home after a busy day at work. The lawn needed to be mowed, and I set about that task. When I entered the house later, my wife was looking out the window, surveying the results of my labor.

"Wow, the lawn looks great. You did a great job."

That simple compliment did amazing things for me. My attitude completely changed. My work was validated. I like compliments—who doesn't? After those few appreciative words, I could have sat and listened to my wife talk about her day at work, the kids, alopecia, or any other issue she needed to talk about. All because of one little compliment, you ask? Absolutely. And over 20 years later, I still get warm feelings just thinking about it. (Yes, that lawn did look good!)

Ladies, try it. One simple, authentic compliment a day. Amazing things could happen to your marriage.

Men, if you find yourself frustrated at your attempts to fix everything presented to you, this free lesson is for you. Remember, she doesn't want you to solve all her problems, she just wants you to hear her thoughts and feelings.

Just to be clear: What I've learned about relationships, I learned the hard way. Throughout 32 years of marriage and

25 years in management, I admit that I attempted to do far too much fixing before I finally learned to do lots of listening.

This little snippet of marriage advice has been brought to you courtesy of a bald eagle on the banks of the Mississippi River. Granted, the above was written after three cups of coffee and with tongue firmly planted in cheek, but it does all have some validity—as you will discover for yourself if you choose to take my advice.

Today's goal was very aggressive—Schoolcraft State Park, named for Henry Rowe Schoolcraft. Schoolcraft and an Ojibwa guide named Ozawindib are credited with charting the headwaters of the Mississippi. (Ozawindib has his own namesake—a lake in Itasca State Park.) I'd have a 32-mile paddle to the state park, but the map promised camping spots directly beside the river. Camping there tonight would also set me up nicely to reach Grand Rapids, Minnesota, on the following day. I was looking forward to enjoying a break in that river town.

Now, though, the only company I had was a massive flock of pelicans congregated on a spit of land in the river. The sight surprised me; for some reason, I had not expected to see pelicans until I reached Louisiana, at the earliest. Unlike the geese, they ignored me and did not disperse as I approached. Apparently, there is safety in numbers.

Between Schoolcraft State Park and Grand Rapids, I'd have to navigate two more dams. Just beyond the smaller town of

Cohasset, the Pokegama Dam held back the river, adjusting water levels for the benefit of both the wild rice crop and spawning fish. Although the dam was more than 10 miles away, I could already detect that the flow of the river had been restricted, and what I had imagined would be a day of floating now became long hours of constant paddling.

I had seen no one all day—a long and lonely day of 10 hours of paddling. Then a small fishing craft appeared around a bend in the river.

To my mind, people always equaled information, and I needed directions to Schoolcraft State Park. I'd covered close to 30 miles, but the river banks had not been friendly and I had spent the entire day on the water in my kayak. The gash on my leg had stopped bleeding but itched constantly. I was exhausted. My body ached from sitting in one position all day. I could not take a chance on missing my camping spot. During the last week, I had noticed that at times the map showed a tent symbol for campgrounds, but none had ever materialized. Either they were out of sight from my position on the river, or I had simply missed them altogether for other reasons.

I did not want to miss this campground.

"How close am I to Schoolcraft?" I called out.

"Two to three miles. It's got one small boat dock. You can't miss it."

How often in life have you heard a similar guarantee? Those are the promises most likely to fail you.

"Looks like you could use some refreshment," observed one fisherman. He tossed a peach across the water into my waiting hands. It was followed by a much-needed bottle of Gatorade.

The peach juice ran down my arms and the Gatorade slaked my thirst as I explained what I was doing. I ended my tale of trials with the comment, "This is actually the first day I haven't feared for my safety."

"Toss that rope over here, and we'll tow you into your campground," they offered.

The voice I heard answering him came from a paddler's head, a head with very little common sense. "I'm sort of a purist. I need to paddle every mile of this river without assistance."

Yes, it was the same voice and feeble mind that had made arrangements the previous evening to skip an entire 15-mile lake crossing. Apparently, this evening the purist in me was rising up and stomping on any further rebellion against its rule.

The fishing boat puttered away, and two words came to my mind: *Stubborn. Stupid.*

Schoolcraft State Park was deserted when I dragged my kayak up the concrete boat ramp. I assembled the wheels on the cart and balanced the kayak on it, then went in search of a camping spot. A pathway through a wooded area led to a series of sites, all empty.

I cannot describe the exhaustion I felt. I can only say that Mark Twain ... well, I was thoroughly disenchanted with the idea of following Tom and Huck down the Mississippi. They had merely hopped aboard a raft and floated down the river. I had to battle for every mile of river I earned.

And now here was another battle. All those flies taking a bite out of me as they flew by on the river—this is where they had actually established residence. They lived here at Schoolcraft, and I had wandered into their banquet hall. Another thought occurred—perhaps they had simply been steering me here all day. Like a sheep to the slaughter. Certainly they had suffered some collateral losses, but they expected that and now their mission was accomplished and here I was, in their lair.

I dislike chemical warfare, but it was the last resort.

As much as I deetest chemicals, I was deetermined to retain as much plasma for the coming days as possible. A misty layer of invincibility settled around me. They were barely deetered, so another toxic cloud was applied. How could they keep eating? Even I could no longer bear to be close to myself.

My phone had vacillated between life and death ever since spending hours in the river, most often showing that red lightning bolt, but occasionally surprising me by coming to life. During one bout of life, I called Ivan as I lay in my fume-filled tent.

I explained that I had been offered a tow that day and had turned it down.

"You are so stupid," he replied.

Only a friend can get away with that brand of truth.

I recalled having thought that word myself earlier in the day. Half of my mind was paralyzed by exhaustion, the other half dead from chemical poisoning, but I managed to focus on all the "s" words that described me that evening. *Stupid* was just a small part of what I was. I was also stinking, stubborn, sad, and snake's-belly low. So low, I had to reach up to touch the bottom. That's low.

In my self-pity, I allowed myself to wallow in regret. Why had I not gone on that bus trip? What had I missed? As I drifted off to sleep, depressed and lonely, I had visions of that bus passing me on the river. And through the chemical headache, I kept hearing echoes of Ivan's words, succinctly assessing my situation.

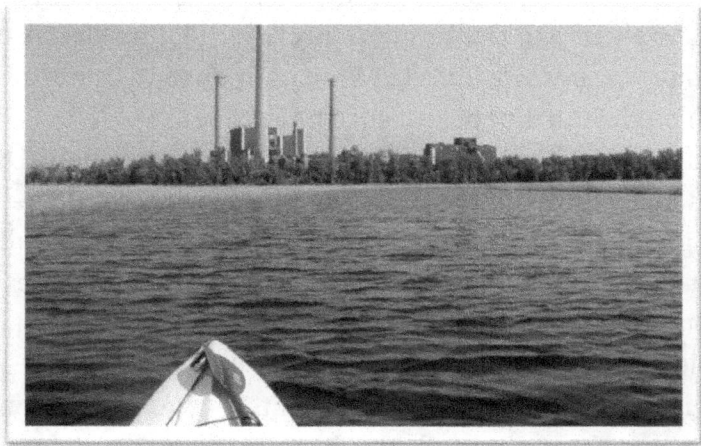

Chapter 16

Was I prepared for this trip? In many ways, I was not. I've already confessed my lack of kayaking experience. I'm not much of a swimmer, and so I'm afraid of deep water. My family had their concerns about this adventure from the very start, but I had promised them I would end it if it was too dangerous. I've always said, though, that you need to face the thing you fear. Do it anyway. You'll learn a lot.

The previous day had been the first day that my life had not been threatened or my safety compromised. It took me eight days to admit that I was not honoring my promise to my family. Instead, I had rationalized—*It's got to get better. This is the hardest part. This stretch today was tough and dangerous, but tomorrow things will surely be different.*

This morning was my ninth morning on the river. If I likened my trip to Dante's trip through the nine circles of hell, this day was my ninth circle. What happened to Dante after the ninth circle? Ah, I'm pretty sure he escaped.

My goal had been Grand Rapids, Minnesota, about 18 river miles away. But I was so desperate for town amenities—a soft bed, good food, and people—that I opted to stop in Cohasset, a small river town only 12 miles away. The aloneness was starting to gnaw at my spirit. Yes, I'd paddle a short day and find lodging in Cohasset.

The river turned into Blackwater Lake, formed by the Pokegama Dam situated just beyond Cohasset. I found the river channel and slowly paddled across the lake toward the town.

An unusual sound startled me. My phone was ringing. Who would possibly be calling me out on this river? In nine days, no one had been able to reach me. They may have attempted to do so, but my phone was dead more often than alive.

The voice was that of my brother-in-law. Another surprise, since he never calls me. He was on that bus traveling across the country. A very private person by nature, he had agreed to join the fracas only out of his love and respect for his spouse.

It would be his first and last bus trip.

As we talked, I imagined him on that bus, trying to maintain his sanity while all about him were losing theirs. While I longed to be in the middle of that bedlam, I was certain he wished he was here on the river with me.

He had felt prompted to call me, he said. He wasn't sure why. Maybe the Holy Spirit had nudged him. Or maybe it was because he was standing at Lake Itasca, and he thought of me.

"What? Did you say Lake Itasca?"

"Yes, that's where I'm standing. Not much of a river is it?"

It was beyond belief. A bus full of sisters, cousins, and friends was that close to me—and I could have been with them.

The connection went kaput, and silence reigned over the river.

As my connection to life outside this river world died, abject loneliness came over me, powerful and palpable. This was loneliness at a level I had never felt before. Perhaps it was the ninth circle of loneliness, about as low and deep as one can go.

Nothing mattered except my family. Some of them were so near—and that suddenly became more important than any other adventure life could offer.

Is it actually possible that we might cross paths?

The hope seemed impossible. But on a whim, I sent a text message to my sister. *Ask Dave where he will cross the river and if he might have room for a stinking cousin.* My cousin Dave was both the bus owner and the driver.

Miraculously, my message went through and a reply came back.

Are you really serious?

My reply was brief and firm. *I'm done.*

My sister replied that she would have Dave check his route and call me.

I was almost across the lake. A bridge loomed ahead, carrying the highway across the river. Several feet before the bridge, a concrete ramp led up out of the water, and I headed for that spot. Cohasset was my destination for the night.

After dragging the kayak up the ramp, I attached the wheels to the cart, loaded up the kayak, and pulled it under a few shade trees. I'd have to find lodging and food. As I contemplated my next move, the phone rang again. It was Dave.

"You sound like the voice of God!" I shouted into the phone.

"I hear you're having quite the time on that river. How serious are you about being picked up?"

"I'm quite done."

"Where are you now?"

"I've just pulled out of the river in a little town called Cohasset."

"Our route has us coming through Cohasset in two hours."

I heard trumpets. I saw red and gold carpets unfurling in my pathway.

"Did you say Cohasset?"

"Yes, Cohasset. We'll be stopping in Bemidji to eat, then on to Cohasset."

"How about the kayak? It's 18 feet long. Will that fit in your luggage bin?"

"That's too big."

"I'll see what I can work out here and call you back."

Energized, with a new life in front of me, I grabbed the tow rope on the kayak and set off for a nearby building. I looked like I was walking an 18-foot pet down the main street of town.

On one corner, the prominent structures were a municipal building and a fire-and-rescue station. I parked the kayak in a corner of the parking lot, facing the street. Across the street was a building I took to be a motel. I walked across the intersection, only to realize it was an apartment complex.

As I was heading back toward my kayak, I must have looked quite lost. A pickup pulled to a stop and the driver asked if he could help me.

I explained my dilemma. I'd been washed out of the river and a bus was stopping in several hours to pick me up and I had no idea what to do with this 18-foot kayak.

Both of the men worked for the town of Cohasset, at the municipal buildings, and they thought there might be room to store the boat with their equipment, although they doubted the manager would give his approval.

The passenger in the pickup lived in Grand Rapids. He offered to load the kayak onto his own truck and take it home with him. I could arrange to have it picked up at a later date.

I reeked of the river, and I asked if there was a place I could clean up. They offered the use of the building's restroom and directed me next door to a gas station where I could get a bite to eat.

Things had certainly taken a turn for the better.

I tried to wash off the worst of the river odors. When I went back to my kayak, preparing to load it onto another pickup, I was informed that the manager of the building had heard of my plight and approved my storing the kayak in the municipal garage. They'd cleared a space for it beside a massive snow-removal grader. I tugged it into the garage and pushed it into its parking spot and thanked everyone profusely.

Could God possibly have worked this out any better? Everything was falling into place. A bus full of family and friends was headed to the very town where I had stopped, and now all of my equipment could be stored here until I found a way to get it home.

My story had traveled quickly through the building, and some came to admire my craft. One man mentioned that he'd never seen such a vessel. I explained that it was a hybrid—a bit of kayak, a bit of canoe.

"There's a guy in town you should talk to," offered the manager. "He's actually my pastor and quite a river paddler himself." As a matter of fact, his pastor had paddled the entire Mississippi River with a few friends. "He's actually written a book about his Mississippi River trip."

At once, gears started turning in my mind, little clicks and clacks ground together and then spit out the realization. Could things possibly get any more incredible?

"That man's name wouldn't be Jim Lewis, would it?"

"Yes, it is. Do you know him?"

"I don't, but I read his book several weeks ago before I left for this trip."

"I'm sure he'd love to talk with you. I'll call him."

Within minutes I was on a phone, talking with the author of a book I had just read about paddling the Mississippi.

Jim and I spoke excitedly for several minutes. I told him about my mishaps in the swamp and the dangerous crossing on Cass Lake.

"That kayak you have is amazing. We've been waiting years for one to wash up on our shore," he said. It turns out the Sea 1 Clipper was the wrong boat for the swamp, but it was probably what saved my life on Cass Lake. Jim was astonished that I came through without the assistance of GPS. "You just did the hardest section of the entire Mississippi River," he told me. "Without GPS. And alone."

"I think God was with me," I replied.

Jim wondered what I planned to do with the kayak. The only solution I could see was to find a trucker back home who might be able to bring it back to Ohio sometime.

"I have a friend who owns a kayak shop in Grand Rapids. Do you want to sell it? I'm sure he would be interested."

I was ready to give everything away. I threw in the marine radio, both paddles, and the machete with the saw blade. Even though I knew I was taking a beating, I gave him an attractive price. I was okay with never seeing the Clipper again.

I also could not imagine ever desiring to return for more river adventures, but Jim offered to go with me if I decided someday to continue on down the Mississippi. It turns out that he is an official river guide. I thanked him and told him I'd contact him if I ever wanted to revisit that quest.

While we were still on the phone, I heard the air brakes outside. Then from around the corner came a rush of familiar humanity and shouts. My sisters and their spouses rushed into the building.

Dear God, what a miracle You have wrought on my behalf.

Following hugs all around, everyone wanted to see the vessel in which I had lived the last nine days, and we all posed for photos around the kayak. The kind folks from the city garage in Cohasset, Minnesota, were also included in the photo.

Conversations were popping everywhere, all at the same time. Words couldn't come out fast enough. I darted from one conversation to another. But there was one question in particular that I wanted to ask: Was Cohasset really on the planned route, or had Dave detoured to pick me up?

The only detour they had taken was into the parking lot. Their planned route had indeed followed the very highway in front of the municipal buildings, within a few feet of where I had parked my kayak.

Applause and shouts of welcome greeted me as I boarded the bus. I would be part of my family's bus adventure after all. Never had anyone failed so miserably and felt so good.

The silence of the river was replaced by loud conversations and bursts of laughter. Instead of being bombarded by flies and mosquitoes, I was bombarded with questions and stories of their own adventure. A sister in front of me, one behind me, and the third across the aisle. This coming home to family must be a small preview of Heaven.

My brother-in-law winked at me from across the aisle.

"This is the best money I've ever spent," he said as he handed me a Bose noise canceling headset. "It blocks out all annoying cousin noises."

"Are you enjoying the trip?" I asked. My sister had reported that he was actually having a good time.

"I hate it! My back hurts, I can't get comfortable in these seats, and it's too loud in here. I'll never do another one of these trips."

I slipped the headphones on. In the midst of the chaos, silence reigned for a few minutes. Then I discovered that this marvel of modern technology also came loaded with music. Melodies from the seventies flowed through. Credence Clearwater Revival sang about being down on some bayou. Other songs from an era so long ago flowed around me, and I drifted off to a place of half sleep and a misty walk down music memory lane.

Nine days, nine circles of misery. And now I was on the chariot sent from God. Going to Heaven on a bus ... bus ... bus. One man's misery is another man's bliss.

My ringing phone brought me back to the bus, rolling away from Cohasset, Minnesota, toward home. The owner of the kayak shop in Grand Rapids was calling because Jim had already told him about my Sea 1 Clipper waiting in the city garage. He wanted to purchase it, sight unseen.

When God works a plan, it's a perfect plan. My plans, not so much.

Chapter 17

God had wrought a miracle on my behalf. Or perhaps not.

Perhaps He did not send that bus for the sole purpose of rescuing His lonely, despairing, bedraggled son from the clutches of the Mississippi River. Perhaps he sent that bus to pick me up and move me back to where He needed me to be. A busload of strangers would not have enticed me to abandon my challenge of the Mississippi, but the persuasion power of my family? God made certain I could not refuse that bus ride home.

Almost immediately after I returned home, my friend Ivan called and suggested lunch. I expected his question.

"Have you thought more about that book?"

I had, indeed. You'll remember that I made a promise to God on Lake Cass—that I would do whatever He wanted me to do if He would just let me live long enough to do it. I was beginning to suspect that God had a reason for washing me out of the weeds and the waves.

I worked for almost a year writing the book, sitting with the couple, listening to their stories and their strong faith. They did indeed have a message for others, a message I think God will use to help many people.

And the same week that the book went to press in the fall of 2014, this faith-filled gentleman went home to be with the Lord he trusted so much.

If I had stayed on the river for another 10 or 12 weeks, the message would never have been written.

So the question is still there: *Did* God wash me out of the river so that I'd get home in time to write a book?

I do know one thing: In my continuing quest to discover exactly what it means to follow Jesus, I've learned that once we sign on, we become partners in Christ's mission in this world. We have work to do. And if God's given us something to do, then we'd best get to it. Sometimes He even rearranges things—performs miracles, if you will—so that we can get the job done.

Do you remember the story of the paralytic who was brought to Jesus? He must have had great friends—four of them actually carried him to the roof of a building and then dug through the roof to lower him into the room right in front of Jesus. The place was so crowded, they couldn't get in the front door.

When I read this account, I wonder how we react when we want to bring someone to Jesus but find the front door blocked. Do we try other approaches? Or do we just give up immediately and go home?

Can you imagine the scene in that crowded house? Folks are all jockeying for a good position to see and hear Jesus. Standing shoulder to shoulder. It's probably getting stuffy and hot in there. Jesus has been preaching God's message, and some of the teachers of religious law who have wiggled their way into the crowd are becoming increasingly steamed at what He's saying. Suddenly, dirt and pieces of the roof start drifting down on their heads. Everybody looks up in amazement, but I think Jesus probably has a little smile on his face. I think He knows.

Here's what's interesting: As that paralytic's pallet came sliding through the roof, down to the floor in front of Him, Jesus saw the faith of *the friends* and He said to the paralyzed man, "My child, your sins are forgiven."

We're never told if the man himself had any faith that Jesus could heal him. It's the faith of the friends and their manual labor that made this healing happen. These guys had faith. I think their faith came because they were followers of Jesus.

114

They were convinced. They knew what He could do. And they were bringing others.

But suppose one of the four had an excuse that day? Suppose he declined being part of a crazy plan to tear up a roof? Suppose he just didn't want to carry his corner of the pallet on which the paralyzed man lay? The other three would have to take up the slack. I don't see that working—with only three carrying, the balance is lost and the dude would probably fall off. Everyone, at his own corner, was necessary to work the plan.

Perhaps God has placed folks in our lives who are paralyzed by pain or despair or lack of faith. As followers of Jesus, we know what He can do to heal lives. But if we don't pick up our corner of the pallet to bring these folks to the Healer, it won't get done or God will have to find someone else to do it.

You may believe that the busload of family coming through the very town I'd landed in was pure coincidence, but I believe God sent that bus to pick me up. He was making it very clear that I was to get home and get busy on that book.

Sometimes God communicates His purposes very clearly. Sometimes there are miracles, events beyond all expectations or belief.

Allow me to tell you about another amazing thing God did in the spring of 2013 as I prepared for what turned out to be my Mississippi misadventure.

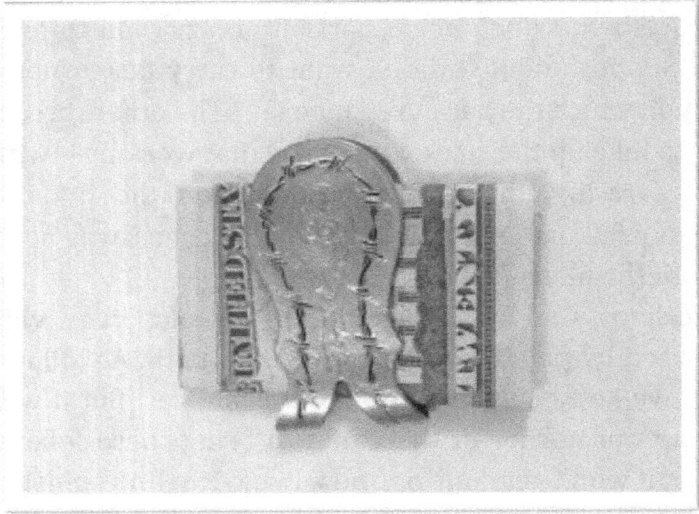

Chapter 18

To appreciate God's plan in this story, you'll need to know something about a particular hostel on the Appalachian Trail.

On a Monday morning in the spring of 2008, I stood on Springer Mountain. This mountain in Georgia is the southern terminus of the Appalachian Trail, a path wandering off into the woods that would take me over 300 mountaintops and through all sorts of other terrain in 14 states to another mountaintop in Maine. My goal was a small sign on top of Mount Katahdin, 2,176 miles away, the northern end of the AT.

MISSISSIPPI *MISADVENTURE*

As I hoisted my pack and took my first steps on the trail, the rain started falling and I was grateful—the raindrops hid the tears streaming down my face.

The future can be frightening, especially so when one has lost the past and given up the present. That was my situation that Monday morning as I walked into the Georgia woods and the unknown future.

What followed was five days of abject misery. Much like my trip on the Mississippi, my fantasies of a pleasant walk in the woods were not the reality I encountered. I was assaulted by rain, high winds, sleet, mud and snow.

I knew of a hostel for hikers near Hiawassee, Georgia, run by a Christian couple. The Blueberry Patch came highly recommended as a place where hikers could find respite from their first week on the trail. I desperately needed a respite.

As I and two other hikers walked over a mountaintop near Dicks Creek Gap, I had a strong enough cell signal to call the hostel. Gary answered my call. He had three bunks available that night, and we took all three. Gary even agreed to come out to the gap and pick us up.

At the hostel, Gary's wife, Lennie, greeted me with a laundry basket and offered to wash my clothes. The hostel had a rustic shower out back, but Lennie told me to use the shower in their own home. A magical appliance turned out to be a shoe dryer. What a pleasure to have dry shoes again! When we were properly reassembled, Gary gave me the keys to his car and told us to drive into town where a fully laden buffet awaited.

My world, burdened down with sadness, had just been suffused with gladness. Without saying one word about God, the Blueberry Patch was a great witness for God. Gary and Lennie were shining examples of what it meant to be a Christian.

The following morning, a bell rang to summon a dozen hungry hikers to breakfast. Around the breakfast table, hikers became acquainted with one another and told stories of how their lives had been interrupted by, well, life.

Most of us had forgotten it was Easter Sunday. Gary had a prayer and spoke about the meaning of Easter. On the trail, hikers rarely go by their given names but choose trail names. I had taken the name *Apostle*. Sure, since I was named Paul that made me Apostle Paul, and yes, several hundred miles north was the town of Damascus, Virginia, to which I was headed, and yes, I did have a few very enlightening encounters along the way. However, I had chosen my trail name because the meaning of the word *apostle* is *one sent forth with a message*. Just as Jesus' apostles were sent out with a message, I wanted to deliver a message to men, especially: *Don't take your spouse and children for granted*. We so often don't appreciate what we have until it's too late.

Gary invited me to go with them to their Easter service.

"We've never had an apostle in our service before," he joked.

I would have loved to go, but I had met my two hiking partners on the trail and they seemed to know what they were doing—and I did not. I was learning from them. They would continue hiking that day, and I did want to stay with them. I told Gary I'd return someday and go to church with him.

I credit the Blueberry Patch with saving my hike. After finishing at the top of Mt. Katahdin, I did write a book, although it turned out to be a far different book than what I had once imagined. On my hike, God spoke to me very clearly and gave me a message to write. I wasn't too enamored with His idea. I didn't think folks would read the book, and if they did, they'd probably think I was crazy. Yet I had a promise from God that He would put *Hiking Through* in the hands of whoever needed the message, so I wrote the book and it was published in 2010.

Following Jesus is sometimes called walking on the straight and narrow pathway, but it often follows a circuitous route. So it was with my return to the Blueberry Patch five years later.

In the summer of 2010, the adventure bug bit me and I pedaled my bicycle nearly 5,000 miles from the farthest corner of Washington State to the opposite corner of the country, Key West, Florida. One of my quirky habits on that trip was to pick up and save all the money I found scattered on roadsides and streets. By the time I reached Florida, a side pocket in my bike pannier was bulging with loose change. But tucked away in the bottom of the pannier, grasped firmly with a silver money clip, was the Big Find.

I was pedaling through Hazel, a stamp-sized burg in Kentucky, when I spied it. The shiny silver money clip lay alongside the highway, showing evidence of having had a rough life on that gravelly road shoulder. I braked to a stop and stuffed it into my pocket without checking the contents. It appeared to be holding several one-dollar bills, and I thought this was the mother lode compared to the nickels, dimes, and pennies I had already picked up.

By that evening I was in Paris, Tennessee, and already comfortably sequestered in my bed when I remembered the money clip. I bounded out of bed and dug it out of my pants pocket. I was right about one thing. It did indeed have three ones in it. The singles were guarding a nest of twenties, who in turn were incubating a plethora of hundreds. Oh, thank you, Jesus.

I had encountered a homeless man on the highway two mornings before, and after hearing his sad story of loss and regret, I had felt compelled to give him a twenty-dollar bill. He wept and said he didn't ask for any money. I informed him it was a free gift. He had done nothing to deserve it. It was just that—a free gift, just as Jesus dying for us was a free gift that we've done nothing to deserve.

It certainly was a good feeling to pedal away from him knowing that I'd helped someone in a small way.

He couldn't repay me, but God could—and as I counted those hundreds in the silver money clip, it seemed God had done just that. Believing that God has a sense of humor, I thanked Him again and remarked that I probably should have given that homeless man 40 bucks.

I joke about that, but I didn't really feel God was rewarding me for my generosity. He had given the money to me to use to bless someone else. So when the cash and I arrived home, I tucked it away in a drawer, and I often asked God for wisdom about where to send it. I received no reply to that question. I did call the local police department and several businesses in the Hazel area, but no one had reported it missing, so they assured me I could keep it in good conscience. It lay in my drawer for three years.

In the spring of 2013, when I was contemplating my Mississippi River expedition and researching kayaks, I realized a good craft would cost a considerable amount of money. It occurred to me that I had a sizable down payment available—that found money, now just wasting away in a drawer.

I'll use it for part of my kayak purchase.

"No, you won't," came a reply from within. The Holy Spirit was alive and well.

"Wish you'd be that clear more often," I mused.

God, I need to know what to do with that money. It could certainly help someone.

At this moment, there was an answer. The Blueberry Patch immediately came to mind. I made a call and set up a visit.

Surprise, surprise. The weekend I scheduled to visit them just happened to be Easter weekend, as it had been the year that I had first stumbled into the Blueberry Patch, weary and worn and ready to give up my hike. Five years later, this Apostle would follow up on a promise he had made; I would go to church with Gary.

I spent a wonderful weekend with Gary and Lennie and hikers coming off the trail. It felt so good to be back in the hiker environment.

121

On that morning, as every morning, Gary opened breakfast with prayer. This prayer was a very personal talk with God, and he called God *Our Daddy*.

Following the meal, I asked if I could speak. I explained how I had found the money in Hazel while on my bike ride, and I thanked Gary and Lennie again for turning my hike around in 2008. Gary graciously received the money and assured me it would be put to good use. Years before, Gary had been a thru-hiker and upon finishing the trail decided to purchase the Blueberry Patch and serve as a mission to other hikers. He moved there from Paris, Tennessee, the very town I had stayed in the night I found the money. At one time, he had delivered papers in nearby Hazel.

Up until that day, I had believed that the reason for my trip was to bless the Blueberry Patch with the money. God had even bigger plans. (He usually does.) The Bible says all things work together for good for those who love the Lord. It also promises that those who seek will find.

After church that morning, I left the hostel and walked several miles on the AT with a few of the hikers I had met.

As I was struggling up one hill, I heard sniffling behind me. A young lady I had seen at breakfast was walking behind me, and she was crying her eyes out.

I felt instant compassion for her; I remembered being on that same trail years earlier and crying out from my own despair. I assured her it was okay to cry; I knew it often got lonely out on the trail.

"That's not why I'm crying," she replied.

"Anything I can help you with?"

122

"Probably not, but here's why I'm losing it this morning. At breakfast, Gary prayed, *God, you are our Daddy.* I so badly want that. My dad left my mom when I was young. I hate my dad. I hate my family. I can't go home because I can't stand them. Matter of fact, I hate my life."

She had recently returned from Afghanistan. Some of her military friends lived in Maine, so she ended up there. She had done some odd jobs but couldn't find peace. One day, a male friend gave her a book as a gift. The guy had no money, so she didn't know how he had come to have the book himself. But he had given it to her, telling her about the author who had hiked the Appalachian Trail in search of peace after suffering a devastating loss.

She did begin to read, but halfway through became angry. The author had indeed discovered peace, that one thing she wanted so badly but could not find. She tossed the book aside in frustration.

But if the writer of that book could find peace on the trail, then maybe she could also. That was why she was here now, still searching for what eluded her. Then Gary's prayer reminded her of what she was missing in life, and the sadness overwhelmed her.

I listened in wonder.

Could it possibly be?

"What was the name of that book you were reading?"

"It was called *Hiking Through.*"

I took a long look at her tear-stained face.

"Do you realize how much God, your Daddy, really loves you?" I asked. "He has put you in the middle of the woods, to the precise minute, with the person who wrote that book!"

There we were, she from Maine and I from Ohio, in the Georgia woods. We looked at each other in astonishment.

I was able to tell her about the love and acceptance Jesus had for her. We exchanged contact information and agreed to stay in touch.

When I returned to the Blueberry Patch for my good-byes before leaving for home, Gary was walking out his side door.

"Gary," I called excitedly, "you won't believe what just happened." I explained how his prayer calling God *our Daddy* had touched the young woman and opened the door to our conversation on the trail.

"Apostle," he said, using my trail name, "you may find this hard to believe as well, but this morning during my prayer and devotional time, the Holy Spirit told me to use *Daddy* in my prayer—and I've *never done that before.*"

God does move in amazing ways His wonders to perform. What if Gary had not upheld his end of the pallet and had not been there for me that first week of my hike? Or what if he had refused to pray that Easter morning as the Spirit directed? What if I had not been obedient and gone to the Blueberry Patch when I felt compelled to? What if I'd never written *Hiking Through* as God wanted it in the first place?

God puts people in our lives who need what we have. Following Jesus means carrying our corner of the pallet. Are we willing to listen to that quiet voice from within asking us to do what might seem crazy? Are we willing to take a risk for God?

God sure took a crazy risk on me, even though my misadventures sometimes end up stuck in the weeds.

GET TO KNOW PAUL STUTZMAN at
www.paulstutzman.com
www.facebook.com/pvstutzman
pstutzman@roadrunner.com

OTHER BOOKS BY PAUL STUTZMAN
The Wandering Home Series (Fiction)
Book One: The Wanderers
Book Two: Wandering Home
Book Three: Wander No More

Adventure Memoir
Hiking Through
One Man's Journey to Peace and Freedom on the Appalachian Trail
Biking Across America
My Coast-to-Coast Adventure and the People I Met Along the Way
Pilgrims (Also published as part of *Stuck in the Weeds*)
On the Camino de Santiago
Hiking Israel (Also titled *The 13th Disciple*)
From Galilee to Jerusalem

Spiritual Memoir
Don't Wait Too Long
The Miracle Journey:
Guideposts to Restoration after Heartbreak and Loss

With Author Serena Miller
More Than Happy: *The Wisdom of Amish Parenting*

The Wanderers

BOOK ONE
OF THE WANDERERS SERIES

PAUL STUTZMAN

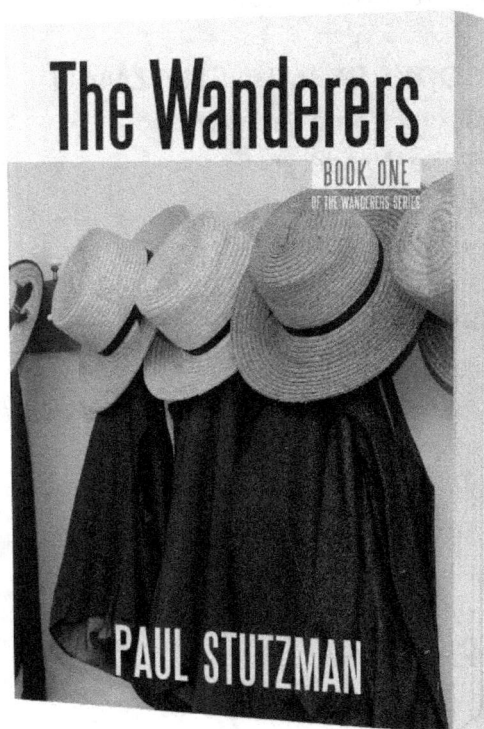

"Young fella, where you frum? Why you running away?"

Leroy L. Jackson, Jr. detected it immediately. Others could see it, too, even if Johnny Miller wouldn't admit it. He was running. Whether he was running from home or toward home, he did not know.

Wandering Home

BOOK TWO
OF THE WANDERERS SERIES

PAUL STUTZMAN

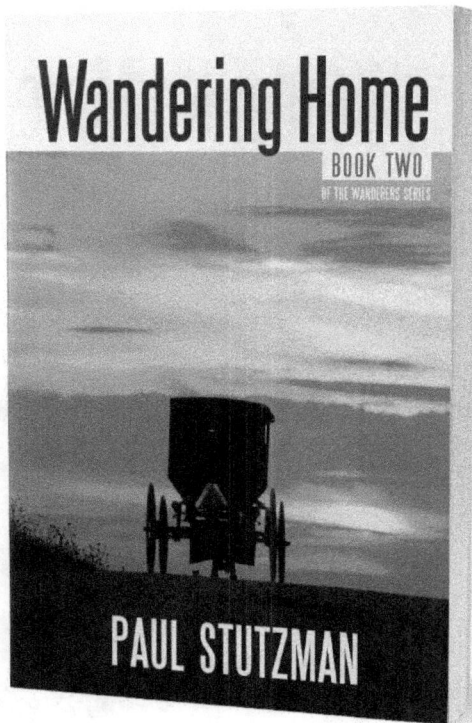

Johnny Miller was twenty-three when he died the first time. The truck hit him as he pedaled along a Texas road, biking across the country in an attempt to find, somehow, somewhere, a new life.

His old life had vanished like a vapor. He thought he had lost everything on the day he lost his dear Annie.But he will lose far more before finally finding the way that leads to home... and life and peace.

Wander No More

BOOK THREE
OF THE WANDERERS SERIES

PAUL STUTZMAN

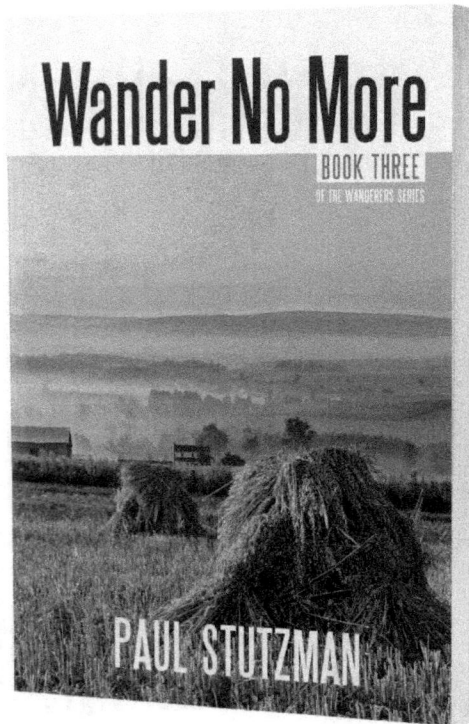

Johnny Miller is back home again, farming the land he loves in a quiet Amish community in Ohio. But although he's not physically wandering, he is still wondering. Wondering why he is restless. Wondering why he feels that some piece of his life is not yet in place. Wondering why, when he was medically "dead," he was met by his wife, who told him his time to enter Heaven had not yet come—he was still needed on earth.

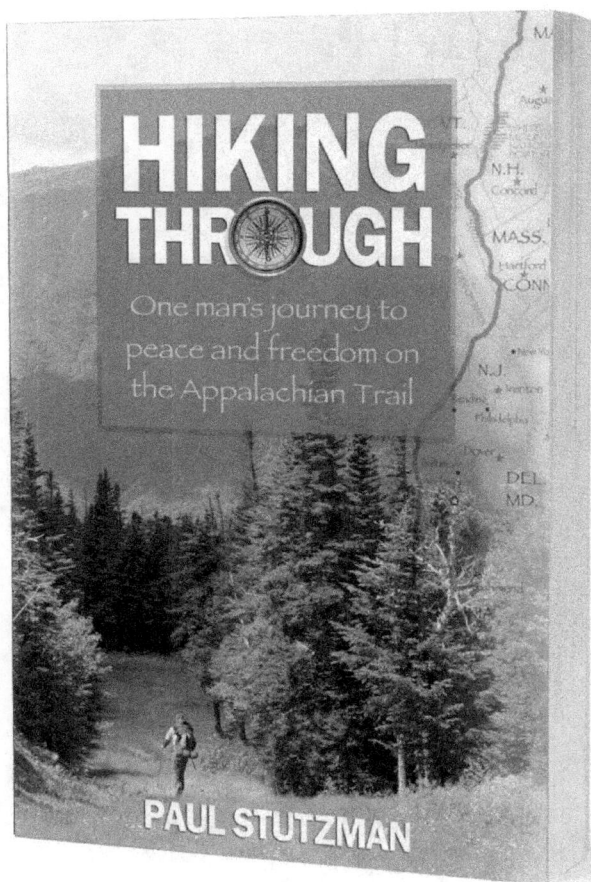

After Paul Stutzman lost his wife to breast cancer, he sensed a tug on his heart—the call to pursue a dream. Paul left his stable career, traveled to Georgia, and took his first steps on the Appalachian Trail. What he learned during the next four and a half months on the trail changed his life—and will change readers' lives as well.

BIKING ACROSS AMERICA

My Coast-to-Coast Adventure and the People I Met Along the Way

PAUL STUTZMAN
Author of *Hiking Through*

Paul Stutzman trades his hiking boots for a bicycle and sets off at Neah Bay, Washington, ending in Key West, Florida, traversing 5,000 miles. Along the way, he encounters nearly every kind of terrain and weather the country has to offer—as well as fascinating people whose stories readers will love.

PILGRIMS

On the Camino de Santiago

PAUL STUTZMAN

Author of *Hiking Through*

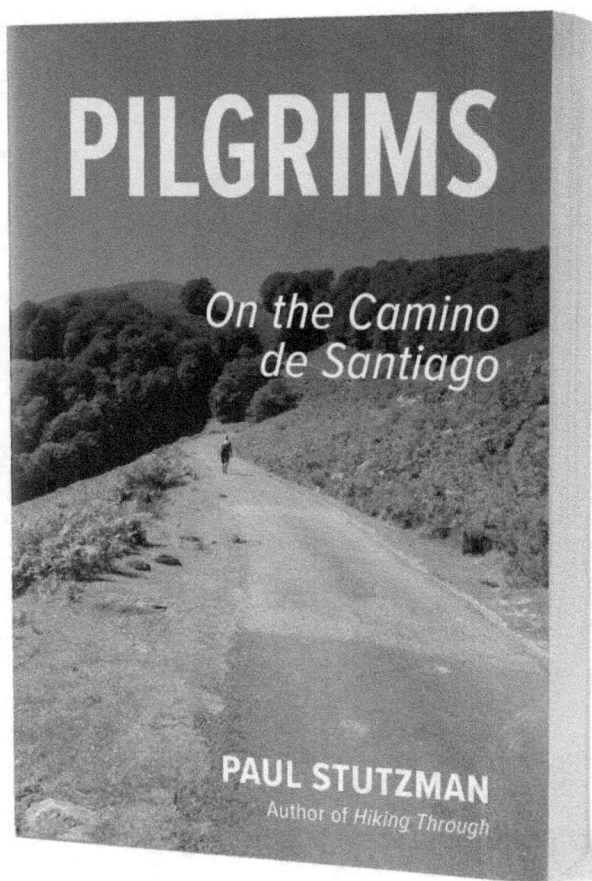

In a pilgrimage to find answers and clarity on personal and faith issues, Paul Stutzman hikes a famous trail in Spain and ponders how choosing to be a disciple of Christ affects the pilgrimage of every believer. (Also published as a segment of *Stuck in the Weeds)*

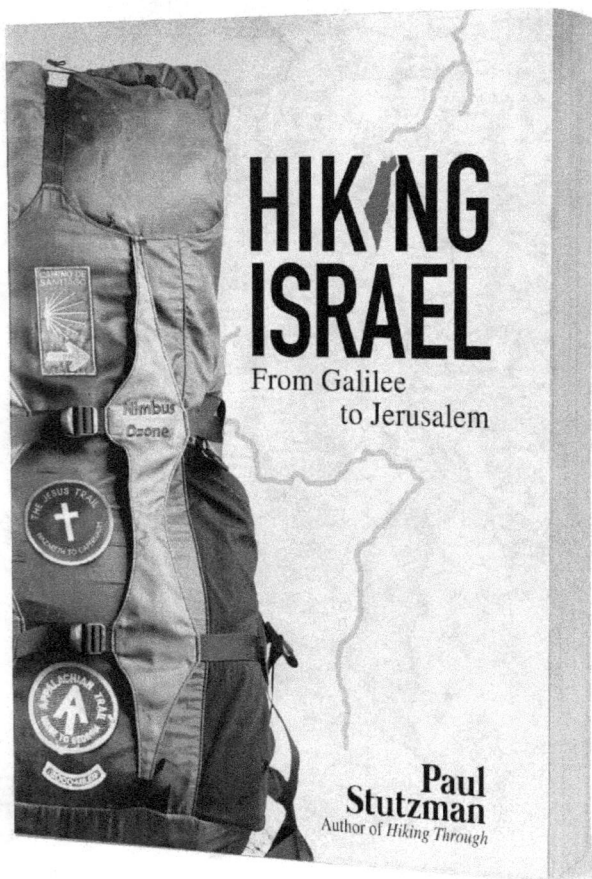

HIK/NG
ISRAEL
From Galilee
to Jerusalem

Paul
Stutzman
Author of *Hiking Through*

On a hike through Israel, Paul Stutzman and his friend Craig visit places that were prominent in the life and ministry of Jesus. Paul is seeking two things: to better know the human Jesus and to find the answer to a question that has puzzled him for years: What does it mean to follow Jesus? Also available under the title *The 13th Disciple*.

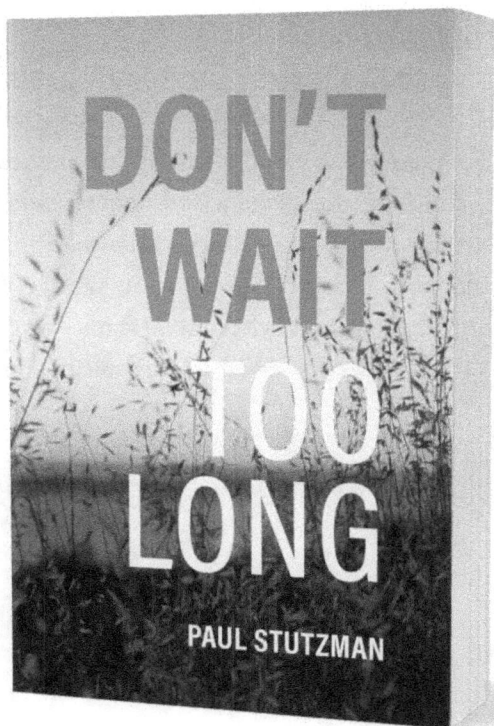

DON'T
WAIT
TOO
LONG

PAUL STUTZMAN

In a deeply personal reflection, Paul writes about two love stories during two years of his life. Don't postpone dreams. Don't wait until the perfect "someday." Paul's message is urgent and applicable to your walk of faith and your human relationships.

COMING IN 2021:

The Miracle Journey:
Guideposts to Restoration after Heartbreak and Loss

"This book is not for everyone," Paul says emphatically. Following his own heartbreak and deep loss, Paul writes to those who have experienced devastation in their lives—loss of loved ones, betrayal, loss of dreams, catastrophic illness, or disaster. How do you survive after life has been shattered? More than that, how is it possible to once again flourish and find hope and joy? Paul invites you along on this spiritual journey as he looks for the miracle.

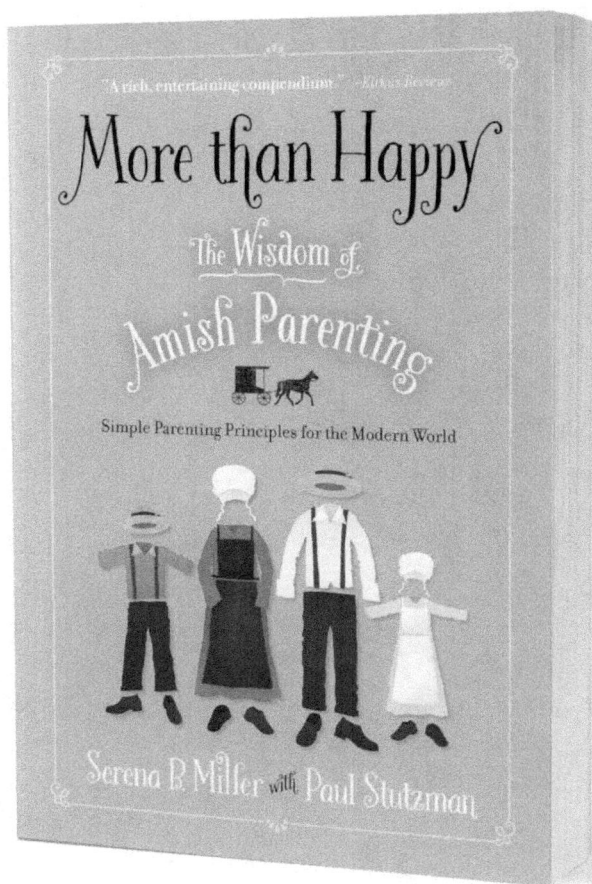

More than Happy
The Wisdom of Amish Parenting
Simple Parenting Principles for the Modern World
Serena B. Miller with Paul Stutzman
"A rich, entertaining compendium." —*Kirkus Reviews*

Author Serena B. Miller talks with Amish parents to discover principles of parenting and family life in Amish homes. Paul Stutzman contributes from his own Amish and Conservative Mennonite upbringing.

With practical takeaways for every family—regardless of religion—on how to raise happy, responsible, productive kids.

www.ingramcontent.com/pod-product-compliance
Lightning Source LLC
LaVergne TN
LVHW021345080426
835508LV00020B/2127